Some Common BASIC Programs Atari® Edition

**Lon Poole
Mary Borchers
Steven Cook**

OSBORNE/McGraw-Hill
Berkeley, California

Disclaimer of Warranties and Limitation of Liabilities

The authors have taken due care in preparing this book and the programs in it, including research, development, and testing to ascertain their effectiveness. The authors and the publishers make no expressed or implied warranty of any kind with regard to these programs nor the supplementary documentation in this book. In no event shall the authors or the publishers be liable for incidental or consequential damages in connection with or arising out of the furnishing, performance, or use of any of these programs.

Atari 400 and Atari 800 are trademarks of Atari, Inc.

Published by
OSBORNE/McGraw-Hill
630 Bancroft Way
Berkeley, California 94710
U.S.A.

For information on translations and book distributors outside of the U.S.A., please write OSBORNE/McGraw-Hill at the above address.

SOME COMMON BASIC PROGRAMS — ATARI® EDITION

1234567890 DLDL 87654321

ISBN 0-931988-53-5

Computer generated image on front cover created by Robert Gotsch.

Special thanks to Cynthia Greever for technical assistance.

Introduction

This book describes a number of programs, written in the Atari® BASIC programming language. These programs perform a variety of common practical tasks.

You can use this book whether or not you know how to write programs in Atari BASIC.

We do not teach you how to program in Atari BASIC; there are many books that do that. But we do describe programs carefully and include user examples with the program listings. So if you are not familiar with Atari BASIC, simply copy the program listings into your computer, then run the programs as illustrated in the examples.

Remarks are included in the listings to help programmers understand how each program works. They will also assist you in identifying parts of programs that you may be able to use in other programs you write. Remark statements precede the line(s) on which they comment. *REM statements should be omitted when you enter programs, since they are ignored by the computer and simply use up memory.*

All programs can be run using a Teletype™ or similar input/output device with a line width as short as 72 characters. If the line width on your output device is less than 72 characters, you may want to alter the print statements within programs that print longer lines.

Certain programs will require additional programming if you use a CRT display or separate printing device for output. If using a CRT, you will probably want to put a pause in some programs after displaying one screenful of data; otherwise, the data will be displayed faster than you can read it. If using a separate printing device for your output, you may need to add print device select statements to the programs.

All programs in this book have been tested, run and listed on an Atari 800™ computer system. They have also been tested and run on an Atari 400™.

Program Errors

If you encounter an error or program difficulty which you believe is not your fault, we would like to hear about it. Please write the publishers, and include the following information:

- A description of the error
- Data entered which caused the error
- A source listing of your program, from your computer (if possible)
- Any corrections you have

Programs

Initial Investment

This program calculates the investment necessary to provide a stated future value in a specified time period. You must enter the future value of the investment, the number of years of investment, the number of compounding periods per year, and the nominal interest rate.

The formula used to calculate the initial investment is as follows:

$$P = \frac{T}{(1 + i/N)^{N \cdot Y}}$$

where: P = initial investment
T = future value
N = number of compounding periods per year
Y = number of years
i = nominal interest rate

Examples:

How much must you invest at 8.5% to produce $10,000.00 at the end of ten years if interest is compounded quarterly?

Merchant Savings wishes to sell a bond that will be worth $5000.00 five years from the purchase date. Interest will be 7.9% compounded daily. How much must the bank charge for the bond?

```
INITIAL INVESTMENT

TOTAL VALUE AFTER Y YEARS? 10000
# OF COMPOUNDING PERIODS PER YEAR? 4
NUMBER OF YEARS? 10
NOMINAL INTEREST RATE? 8.5
INITIAL INVESTMENT = $4312.38

MORE DATA? (1=YES, 0=NO)? 1

TOTAL VALUE AFTER Y YEARS? 5000
# OF COMPOUNDING PERIODS PER YEAR? 365
NUMBER OF YEARS? 5
NOMINAL INTEREST RATE? 7.9
INITIAL INVESTMENT = $3368.59

MORE DATA? (1=YES, 0=NO)? 0


5 GRAPHICS 0
10 PRINT "INITIAL INVESTMENT"
20 PRINT
29 REM - STATEMENTS 30 TO 100 REQUEST USER INPUT
30 PRINT "TOTAL VALUE AFTER Y YEARS";
40 INPUT T
50 PRINT "# OF COMPOUNDING PERIODS PER YEAR";
60 INPUT N
70 PRINT "NUMBER OF YEARS";
80 INPUT Y
```

```
90 PRINT "NOMINAL INTEREST RATE";
100 INPUT I
108 REM - CALCULATE INTEREST RATE PER PERIOD
109 REM - CONVERT FROM PERCENT TO DECIMAL
110 I=I/N/100
119 REM - CALCULATE  INITIAL INVESTMENT BY FORMULA
120 P=T/(1+I)^(N*Y)
129 REM - ROUND OFF TO NEAREST CENT, PRINT
130 PRINT "INITIAL INVESTMENT = $";
135 PRINT INT(P*100+0.5)/100
140 PRINT
149 REM - RESTART OR END PROGRAM? USER INPUT REQUIRED
150 PRINT "MORE DATA? (1=YES, 0=NO)";
160 INPUT X
170 IF X=1 THEN 20
180 END
```

OPTION

The program above allows you to enter a period of investment of whole years and decimal parts only. You may wish to enter the period of investment in years and months rather than just years. The program changes necessary are listed following the example below.

Example:

Mary wishes to invest a sum in a savings bank. In three years and eight months she would like to have $4000.00 in her account. If 8% interest is compounded monthly, what amount must Mary invest?

```
INITIAL INVESTMENT

TOTAL VALUE AFTER Y YEARS? 4000
# OF COMPOUNDING PERIODS PER YEAR? 12
NUMBER OF YEARS, MONTHS? 3,8
NOMINAL INTEREST RATE? 8
INITIAL INVESTMENT = $2986

MORE DATA? (1=YES, 0=NO)? 0

1 REM - OPTION 70-85
5 GRAPHICS 0
10 PRINT "INITIAL INVESTMENT"
.
.
60 INPUT N
70 PRINT "NUMBER OF YEARS, MONTHS";
80 INPUT Y0,M
84 REM - CALCULATE YEARS FROM YEARS AND MONTHS
85 Y=(12*Y0+M)/12
90 PRINT "NOMINAL INTEREST RATE";
.
.
180 END
```

Minimum Investment for Withdrawals

This program calculates the minimum investment required to allow regular withdrawals over a specified time period. The amount calculated is dependent upon the amount of each withdrawal, the number of withdrawals per year, the number of years, and the nominal interest rate on the investment. All withdrawals are equal.

Only the least amount necessary for your investment is calculated; the program assumes a balance of $0.00 to be left at the end of the time period. Any investment larger than the amount calculated will also enable you to withdraw the desired amount, but leave a remaining balance.

Assuming that interest is compounded with each withdrawal, the calculation is based on the following formula:

$$P = \frac{R \cdot N}{i} \left(1 - \frac{1}{(1 + i/N)^{N \cdot Y}} \right)$$

where: P = initial investment
R = amount of regular withdrawal
i = nominal interest rate
N = number of withdrawals per year
Y = number of years

Example:

How much must you invest at 6% interest to allow monthly withdrawals of $100.00 for five years?

```
MINIMUM INVESTMENT FOR WITHDRAWALS

AMOUNT OF WITHDRAWALS? 100
NOMINAL INTEREST RATE? 6
# OF WITHDRAWALS PER YEAR? 12
NUMBER OF YEARS? 5
MINIMUM INVESTMENT = $5172.56

MORE DATA? (1=YES, 0=NO)? 0
```

```
5 GRAPHICS 0
10 PRINT "MINIMUM INVESTMENT FOR WITHDRAWALS"
20 PRINT
29 REM - STATEMENTS 30 TO 100 REQUEST USER INPUT
30 PRINT "AMOUNT OF WITHDRAWALS";
40 INPUT R
50 PRINT "NOMINAL INTEREST RATE";
60 INPUT I
70 PRINT "# OF WITHDRAWALS PER YEAR";
80 INPUT N
90 PRINT "NUMBER OF YEARS";
100 INPUT Y
109 REM - CONVERT FROM PERCENT TO DECIMAL
110 I=I/100
119 REM - CALCULATE MINIMUM INVESTMENT BY FORMULA
```

```
120 P=R*N/I*(1-1/((1+I/N)^(N*Y)))
129 REM - ROUND OFF TO NEAREST CENT, PRINT
130 PRINT "MINIMUM INVESTMENT = $";
135 PRINT INT(100*P+0.5)/100
140 PRINT
149 REM - RESTART OR END PROGRAM? USER INPUT REQUIRED
150 PRINT "MORE DATA? (1=YES, 0=NO)";
160 INPUT X
170 IF X=1 THEN 20
180 END
```

OPTION

It may be more convenient to enter the term of investment in years and months rather than years. The necessary program changes are listed following the example below.

Example:

Tony withdrew $250.00 monthly for six years and five months. How much was his initial investment at 6% interest?

```
MINIMUM INVESTMENT FOR WITHDRAWALS

AMOUNT OF WITHDRAWALS? 250
NOMINAL INTEREST RATE? 6
# OF WITHDRAWALS PER YEAR? 12
NUMBER OF YEARS, MONTHS? 6,5
MINIMUM INVESTMENT = $15944.82

MORE DATA? (1=YES, 0=NO)? 0

1 REM - OPTION 90-105
5 GRAPHICS 0
10 PRINT "MINIMUM INVESTMENT FOR WITHDRAWALS"
  :
80 INPUT N
90 PRINT "NUMBER OF YEARS, MONTHS";
100 INPUT YO,M
104 REM - CALCULATE YEARS FROM YEARS AND MONTHS
105 Y=(12*YO+M)/12
109 REM - CONVERT FROM PERCENT TO DECIMAL
  :
180 END
```

Nominal Interest Rate on Investments

This program calculates the nominal interest rate for a known initial investment which amounts to a known future value in a specified period of time. The nominal interest rate is usually subdivided for compounding purposes.

"Nominal Interest Rate" is based on the following formula:

$$i = N\,(T/P)^{\frac{1}{N\cdot Y}} - N$$

where: i = nominal interest rate
P = initial investment
T = future value
N = number of compounding periods per year
Y = number of years

The nominal interest rate is expressed as a yearly rate even though the interest rate used when compounding interest is i/N. The nominal interest rate will be less than the effective interest rate when interest is compounded more than once a year. This is because the nominal rate stated does not take into account interest compounded on interest earned in earlier periods of each year. For example, the schedule of earned interest on $100.00 at 5% compounded quarterly would be:

Period	Balance	$\frac{i/100}{N}$	Interest	New Balance
1	$100.00 • 0.0125 =		$1.25	$101.25
2	$101.25 • 0.0125 =		$1.27	$102.52
3	$102.52 • 0.0125 =		$1.28	$103.80
4	$103.80 • 0.0125 =		$1.30	$105.10

The *effective* interest rate in the example is 5.1%, although the *nominal* rate is 5%.

Examples:

Dick invests $945.00 in a savings bank. Four and a half years later his investment amounts to $1309.79. If interest is compounded monthly, what is the nominal interest rate offered by the bank?

Jane invests $3000.00. Ten years later she has earned $1576.00 in interest. If interest is compounded each month, what is the nominal interest rate on the account?

```
NOMINAL INTEREST RATE ON INVESTMENTS

PRINCIPAL? 945
TOTAL VALUE? 1309.79
NUMBER OF YEARS? 4.5
# OF COMPOUNDING PERIODS PER YEAR? 12
NOMINAL INTEREST RATE =7.276104%

MORE DATA? (1=YES, 0=NO)? 1
PRINCIPAL? 3000
TOTAL VALUE? 4576
NUMBER OF YEARS? 10
# OF COMPOUNDING PERIODS PER YEAR? 12
```

```
NOMINAL INTEREST RATE =4.229544%

MORE DATA? (1=YES, 0=NO)? 0

5 GRAPHICS 0
10 PRINT "NOMINAL INTEREST RATE ON INVESTMENTS"
20 PRINT
29 REM - STATEMENTS 30 TO 100 REQUEST USER INPUT
30 PRINT "PRINCIPAL";
40 INPUT P
50 PRINT "TOTAL VALUE";
60 INPUT T
70 PRINT "NUMBER OF YEARS";
80 INPUT Y
90 PRINT "# OF COMPOUNDING PERIODS ";
95 PRINT "PER YEAR";
100 INPUT N
109 REM - CALCULATE NOMINAL INTEREST RATE BY FORMULA, PRINT
110 I2=N*((T/P)^(1/(N*Y))-1)*100
120 PRINT "NOMINAL INTEREST RATE =";
121 PRINT I2;"%"
130 PRINT
139 REM - RESTART OR END PROGRAM? USER INPUT REQUIRED
140 PRINT "MORE DATA? (1=YES, 0=NO)";
150 INPUT X
160 IF X=1 THEN 20
170 END
```

Effective Interest Rate on Investments

This program calculates the effective interest rate for a known initial investment which amounts to a known future value in a specified period of time. This rate expresses the actual rate of interest earned annually on the investment.

The effective interest rate is calculated by the following formula:

$$\text{effective} \atop \text{interest rate} = \left(\frac{\text{future value}}{\text{initial investment}} \right)^{1/\text{years}} - 1$$

You may calculate the effective interest rate on amounts you have already invested and accrued interest upon. Or you may calculate the effective interest rate necessary to enable a principal to reach a hypothetical value in a specified amount of time. For instance, if you invest $5000.00 in a bank and desire $6800.00 after six years, you will predict the effective interest rate the bank must pay in order to achieve this.

"Effective Interest Rate" may also be used to calculate the effective percent of depreciation of an investment. Take your car, for example. If you bought it for $7534.00 and sold it for $3555.00 three years later, you will find that its actual depreciation (a negative interest rate) was approximately 22% each year.

Examples:

Dick deposits $945.00 in a savings bank. Four and a half years later his account has $1309.79. What actual percent of his initial investment did the bank pay annually?

Jane bought her car in 1970 for $7534.84 and sold it in 1973 for $3555.00. What was its effective rate of depreciation?

```
EFFECTIVE INTEREST RATE ON INVESTMENTS

INITIAL INVESTMENT? 945
TOTAL VALUE AFTER Y YEARS? 1309.79
NUMBER OF YEARS? 4.5
ANNUAL INTEREST RATE =7.523751%

MORE DATA? (1=YES, 0=NO)? 1

INITIAL INVESTMENT? 7534.84
TOTAL VALUE AFTER Y YEARS? 3555
NUMBER OF YEARS? 3
ANNUAL INTEREST RATE =-22.150613%

MORE DATA? (1=YES, 0=NO)? 0


5 GRAPHICS 0
10 PRINT "EFFECTIVE INTEREST RATE ON INVESTMENTS"
20 PRINT
29 REM - STATEMENTS 30 TO 80 REQUEST USER INPUT
30 PRINT "INITIAL INVESTMENT";
40 INPUT P
50 PRINT "TOTAL VALUE AFTER Y YEARS";
60 INPUT T
```

```
70 PRINT "NUMBER OF YEARS";
80 INPUT Y
89 REM - CALCULATE EFFECTIVE INTEREST RATE, PRINT
90 PRINT "ANNUAL INTEREST RATE =";
99 REM - PRINT BLANK LINE TO SEPARATE DATA FROM QUESTION
100 PRINT ((T/P)^(1/Y)-1)*100;"%"
109 PRINT
110 REM - RESTART OR END PROGRAM? USER INPUT REQUIRED
120 PRINT "MORE DATA? (1=YES, 0=NO)";
130 INPUT X
140 IF X=1 THEN 20
150 END
```

Earned Interest Table

This program calculates and prints an earned interest table for investments. The schedule contains the following outputs:

1. Periodic balance
2. Interest accumulated between two periods
3. Total interest accumulated
4. Effective interest rate

These outputs may be calculated for a single investment or for an initial investment with regular deposits or withdrawals. If the table is to be tabulated for a single investment, you must provide the amount of the initial investment, the nominal interest rate, and the number of compounding periods per year. Your new balance will be printed a maximum of four times per year. If interest is compounded less than four times per year, your new balance will be posted with each interest computation.

If the table is tabulated for regular deposits or withdrawals, you must provide the amount of the initial investment, the nominal interest rate, the number of deposits or withdrawals per year, and their amount. In this case it is assumed that interest is compounded daily (360-day year). Your new balance will be printed at each deposit or withdrawal.

Examples:

Sally invests $2000.00 at 9.5% in a trust fund for ten years. Interest is compounded monthly. What is her yearly balance and earned interest for the last two years?

John deposits $1000.00 at 8% in a passbook savings account. From each monthly paycheck $50.00 is deposited in this account. What is the earned interest table for the first year of this account?

Ted deposits $1000.00 at 8% in his savings. Each quarter he withdraws $150.00. What is the earned interest table for the first year of this account?

```
EARNED INTEREST TABLE

PRINCIPAL? 2000
NOMINAL INTEREST RATE? 9.5
# OF DEPOSITS/WITHDRAWALS PER YEAR? 0
# OF COMPOUNDING PERIODS PER YEAR? 12
START WITH WHAT YEAR? 9
END PRINTING WITH WHAT YEAR? 10
```

```
          EARNED INTEREST TABLE
    PRINCIPAL $2000  AT 9.5% NOMINAL FOR 10 YEARS
       EFFECTIVE INTEREST RATE 9.92% PER YEAR
```

YEAR	BALANCE	INTEREST	ACCUM. INT.
9	4365.87	2365.86	2365.87
	4470.38	104.51	2470.38
	4577.39	107.01	2577.39
	4686.97	109.58	2686.97
10	4799.17	112.2	2799.17
	4914.05	114.88	2914.05
	5031.68	117.63	3031.68
	5152.13	120.45	3152.13

```
CHANGE DATA AND RECOMPUTE?
(1=YES, 0=NO)? 1

PRINCIPAL? 1000
NOMINAL INTEREST RATE? 8
# OF DEPOSITS/WITHDRAWALS PER YEAR? 12
AMOUNT OF DEPOSIT/WITHDRAWAL? 50
START WITH WHAT YEAR? 1
END PRINTING WITH WHAT YEAR? 1
```

                    EARNED INTEREST TABLE
          PRINCIPAL $1000   AT 8% NOMINAL FOR 1 YEAR
       REGULAR DEPOSITS/WITHDRAWALS $50 12 TIMES PER YEAR
            EFFECTIVE INTEREST RATE   8.33% PER YEAR

YEAR	BALANCE	INTEREST	ACCUM.INT.
1	1056.7	6.7	6.7
	1113.78	7.08	13.78
	1171.24	7.46	21.24
	1229.08	7.84	29.08
	1287.32	8.23	37.32
	1345.94	8.62	45.94
	1404.95	9.01	54.95
	1464.36	9.41	64.36
	1524.17	9.8	74.17
	1584.37	10.2	84.37
	1644.98	10.61	94.98
	1706	11.01	106

```
CHANGE DATA AND RECOMPUTE?
(1=YES, 0=NO)? 0
5 GRAPHICS 0
6 DIM W$(1)
10 PRINT "EARNED INTEREST TABLE"
20 PRINT
29 REM - STATEMENTS 30 TO 230 REQUEST USER INPUT
30 PRINT "PRINCIPAL";
40 INPUT P
50 PRINT "NOMINAL INTEREST RATE";
60 INPUT I
69 REM - CONVERT PERCENT TO DECIMAL
70 I=I/100
80 PRINT "# OF DEPOSITS/WITHDRAWALS PER YEAR";
90 INPUT N1
99 REM - DON'T ASK FOR AMOUNT IF FREQUENCY IS ZERO
100 IF N1=0 THEN 160
108 REM - DEPOSITS ARE ENTERED AS A POSITIVE NUMBER
109 REM - WITHDRAWALS ARE ENTERED AS A NEGATIVE NUMBER
110 PRINT "AMOUNT OF DEPOSIT/WITHDRAWAL";
120 INPUT R
129 REM - INTEREST IS COMPOUNDED DAILY
130 N=360
139 REM - PRINT AT EACH DEPOSIT/WITHDRAWAL
140 L2=N1
150 GOTO 200
```

```
160 PRINT "# OF COMPOUNDING PERIODS PER YEAR";
170 INPUT N
180 N1=0
189 REM - PRINT FOUR TIMES EACH YEAR
190 L2=4
200 PRINT "START WITH WHAT YEAR";
210 INPUT X
220 PRINT "END PRINTING WITH WHAT YEAR";
230 INPUT Y
239 REM - START PRINTING AT THE BEGINNING OF A YEAR
240 X=INT(X)
249 REM - INITIATE RUNNING TOTALS
250 BO=P
260 I1=0
270 I2=0
280 I3=0
290 K=66:REM FORCE PAGE TO START
300 P1=4
310 FOR JO=1 TO INT(Y)
313 REM - START PRINTING?
314 REM - IF FIRST YEAR, SKIP CHECK FOR FULL SCREEN
315 IF JO=X THEN 370
320 IF JO<X THEN 480
330 IF K<22 THEN 470
338 REM - FULL SCREEN (22 LINES)?
339 REM - IF YES, CLEAR SCREEN, PRINT HEADINGS
342 REM - WAIT FOR OPERATOR CUE TO GO TO NEXT SCREEN
344 PRINT "PRESS 'RETURN' TO CONTINUE";
345 INPUT W$
370 K=10
375 GRAPHICS 0
376 POSITION 0,23
380 PRINT "          EARNED  INTEREST  TABLE"
385 PRINT
390 PRINT "PRINCIPAL $";P;"   AT ";I*100;"% NOMINAL"
395 PRINT "FOR ";Y;" YEARS"
396 PRINT
399 REM - SKIP DEPOSIT/WITHDRAWAL HEADING IF THERE ARE NONE
400 IF N1=0 THEN 430
410 PRINT "REGULAR DEPOSITS/WITHDRAWALS $";R
415 PRINT "              ";N1;" TIMES PER YEAR"
416 PRINT
419 REM - K COUNTS THE NUMBER OF PRINTED LINES PER PAGE
420 K=K+1
430 PRINT "EFFECTIVE INTEREST RATE";
435 PRINT INT((100*((1+I/N)^N-1))*100+0.5)/100;
436 PRINT "% PER YEAR"
440 PRINT
450 PRINT "YEAR  BALANCE    INTEREST     ACCUM.INT."
459 REM - CALCULATE INTEREST
460 PRINT
469 REM - PRINT YEAR NUMBER
470 PRINT JO;
480 L1=1
490 N2=1
```

```
500 P2=1
510 FOR J1=1 TO N
519 REM - DEPOSIT/WITHDRAW ANY MORE THIS YEAR?
520 IF N2>N1 THEN 560
529 REM - TIME TO MAKE DEPOSIT/WITHDRAWAL?
530 IF N2/N1>J1/N THEN 560
539 REM - CALCULATE NEW BALANCE
540 B0=B0+R
549 REM - COUNT DEPOSITS/WITHDRAWALS MADE PER YEAR
550 N2=N2+1
560 B2=B0*(1+I/N)
569 REM - I1=AMOUNT INTEREST WITH EACH COMPOUNDING PERIOD
570 I1=B2-B0
579 REM - I3=AMOUNT INTEREST ACCUMULATED BETWEEN POSTINGS
580 I3=I3+I1
589 REM - I2=TOTAL INTEREST ACCUMULATED TO DATE
590 I2=I2+I1
599 REM - ROUND AT INTEREST POSTING TIME
600 IF P2/P1>J1/N THEN 640
610 I2=INT(I2*100+0.5)/100
620 B2=INT(B2*100+0.5)/100
630 P2=P2+1
639 REM - YEAR TO START PRINTING?
640 IF J0<X THEN 710
649 REM - TIME TO PRINT A LINE?
650 IF J1/N<L1/L2 THEN 710
660 L1=L1+1
670 POSITION 6,23
672 PRINT INT(B2*100+0.5)/100;
673 POSITION 20,23
674 PRINT INT(I3*100+0.5)/100;
675 POSITION 30,23
676 PRINT INT(I2*100+0.5)/100
679 REM - INTEREST POSTED, REINITIALIZE INTEREST ACCUMULATED BETWEEN
POSTINGS
680 I3=0
710 B0=B2
719 REM - NO MORE LINES TO PRINT IN LAST YEAR?
720 IF J0+J1/N-1>Y THEN 780
730 NEXT J1
739 REM - START PRINTING?
740 IF J0<X THEN 770
750 PRINT
760 K=K+1+L2
770 NEXT J0
780 PRINT
789 REM - RESTART OR END PROGRAM? USER INPUT REQUIRED
790 PRINT "CHANGE DATA AND RECOMPUTE?"
795 PRINT "(1=YES, 0=NO)";
800 INPUT Z
810 PRINT
820 IF Z=1 THEN 20
830 END
```

Depreciation Rate

This program calculates the annual depreciation rate of an investment. You must provide the original price of the item, its resale price, and its age in years.

The depreciation rate is calculated by the following formula:

$$\text{depreciation rate} = 1 - \left(\frac{\text{resale price}}{\text{original price}}\right)^{1/\text{age}}$$

Example:

Joan bought her car for $4933.76 and sold it for $2400.00 three years later. What was its actual depreciation rate?

```
DEPRECIATION RATE

ORIGINAL PRICE? 4933.76
RESALE PRICE? 2400
YEARS? 3
DEPRECIATION RATE =21.354%

MORE DATA? (1=YES, 0=NO)? 0

5 GRAPHICS 0
10 PRINT "DEPRECIATION RATE"
20 PRINT
30 PRINT "ORIGINAL PRICE";
40 INPUT P
50 PRINT "RESALE PRICE";
60 INPUT T
70 PRINT "YEARS";
80 INPUT Y
89 REM - CALCULATE DEPRECIATION RATE BY FORMULA, CONVERT TO PERCENT
90 D=100*(1-(T/P)^(1/Y))
100 PRINT "DEPRECIATION RATE =";
105 PRINT INT(1000*D+0.5)/1000;"%"
110 PRINT
119 REM - RESTART OR END PROGRAM? USER INPUT REQUIRED
120 PRINT "MORE DATA? (1=YES, 0=NO)";
130 INPUT X
140 IF X=1 THEN 20
150 END
```

Depreciation Amount

This program calculates the dollar amount depreciated within a given year for a depreciating investment. You must provide the original price of the investment, its depreciation rate, and the year of depreciation.

The depreciation amount is calculated by the following formula:

$$D = P \cdot i \cdot (1 - i)^{Y-1}$$

where: D = depreciation amount
P = original price
i = depreciation rate
Y = year of depreciation

Examples:

Joan bought her car for $4933.76. Her model car depreciates at an average annual rate of 21%. What amount has the car depreciated in each of the first three years she has owned it?

Joan is also concerned about the depreciation of the tape deck in her car. It cost her $155.00 two years ago, and has a depreciation rate of 22%. How much will its value decline in the third year?

```
DEPRECIATION AMOUNT

ORIGINAL PRICE? 4933.76
DEPRECIATION RATE? 21
--(ENTER YEAR=0 TO END)--
YEAR? 1
DEPRECIATION = $1036.09

YEAR? 2
DEPRECIATION = $818.51

YEAR? 3
DEPRECIATION = $646.62

YEAR? 0
MORE DATA? (1=YES,0=NO)? 1

ORIGINAL PRICE? 155
DEPRECIATION RATE? 22
--(ENTER YEAR=0 TO END)--
YEAR? 3
DEPRECIATION = $20.75

YEAR? 0
MORE DATA? (1=YES,0=NO)? 0

5 GRAPHICS 0
10 PRINT "DEPRECIATION AMOUNT"
20 PRINT
30 PRINT "ORIGINAL PRICE";
40 INPUT P
50 PRINT "DEPRECIATION RATE";
```

```
60 INPUT I
69 REM - CONVERT FROM PERCENT TO DECIMAL
70 I=I/100
80 PRINT "--(ENTER YEAR=0 TO END)--"
90 PRINT "YEAR";
100 INPUT Y
109 REM - THROUGH CALCULATING FOR THIS ITEM?
110 IF Y=0 THEN 160
119 REM - CALCULATE DEPRECIATION AMOUNT BY FORMULA
120 D=P*I*(1-I)^(Y-1)
129 REM - ROUND OFF TO NEAREST CENT, PRINT
130 PRINT "DEPRECIATION = $";
135 PRINT INT(D*100+0.5)/100
140 PRINT
149 REM - RETURN FOR NEXT YEAR NUMBER
150 GOTO 90
159 REM - RESTART OR END PROGRAM?
160 PRINT "MORE DATA? (1=YES, 0=NO)";
170 INPUT X
180 IF X=1 THEN 20
190 END
```

Salvage Value

This program calculates the salvage value of an item at the end of a given year. It is necessary for you to provide the age of the item, its original price, and its depreciation rate.

The salvage value is obtained by the following formula:

$$S = P(1 - i)^Y$$

where: S = salvage value
P = original price
i = depreciation rate
Y = age in years

Example:

What is the salvage value of Joan's car it if is three years old, she bought it for $4933.76, and it depreciates 21% annually? What would its salvage value be next year?

Joan's tape deck is two years old. What is the its salvage value if it cost $155.00 originally and depreciates at a rate of 22%?

```
SALVAGE VALUE

ORIGINAL PRICE? 4933.76
DEPRECIATION RATE? 21
--(ENTER YEAR=0 TO END)--
YEARS? 3
VALUE = $2432.54

YEARS? 4
VALUE = $1921.7

YEARS? 0
MORE DATA? (1=YES, 0=NO)? 1

ORIGINAL PRICE? 155
DEPRECIATION RATE? 22
--(ENTER YEAR=0 TO END)--
YEARS? 2
VALUE = $94.3

YEARS? 0
MORE DATA? (1=YES, 0=NO)? 0

5 GRAPHICS 0
10 PRINT "SALVAGE VALUE"
20 PRINT
30 PRINT "ORIGINAL PRICE";
40 INPUT P
50 PRINT "DEPRECIATION RATE";
60 INPUT I
70 PRINT "--(ENTER YEAR=0 TO END)--"
80 PRINT "YEARS";
```

```
90  INPUT Y
99  REM - CALCULATE ANOTHER SALVAGE VALUE?
100 IF Y=0 THEN 140
108 REM - CALCULATE SALVAGE VALUE BY FORMULA, ROUND OFF, PRINT
109 REM - DEPRECIATION RATE CONVERTED TO DECIMAL FOR USE IN CALCULATIONS
110 PRINT "VALUE = $";
115 PRINT INT(100*P*(1-I/100)^Y+0.5)/100
120 PRINT
129 REM - RETURN FOR NEXT YEAR NUMBER
130 GOTO 80
139 REM - RESTART OR END PROGRAM? USER INPUT REQUIRED
140 PRINT "MORE DATA? (1=YES, 0=NO)";
150 INPUT X
160 IF X=1 THEN 20
170 END
```

Discount Commercial Paper

This program calculates the amount of discount and net cost of a discounted commercial paper. You must provide the future value of the paper, the discount rate and the number of days to maturity.

The formulas used to calculate the discount and cost are as follows:

$$\text{discount} = T \cdot \frac{D}{100} \cdot \frac{N}{360}$$

$$\text{cost} = T - \text{discount}$$

where: T = total future value
D = discount rate
N = number of days to maturity

Example:

Canning Corporation purchases a $625,000.00 commercial paper due in 60 days at 5.4%. What is the discount and cost?

```
DISCOUNT COMMERCIAL PAPER

FUTURE VALUE? 625000
DISCOUNT RATE? 5.4
DAYS TO MATURITY? 60
DISCOUNT = $5625
    COST = $619375

MORE DATA? (1=YES, 0=NO)? 0

5 GRAPHICS 0
10 PRINT "DISCOUNT COMMERCIAL PAPER"
20 PRINT
29 REM - STATEMENTS 30 TO 90 REQUEST USER INPUT
30 PRINT "FUTURE VALUE";
40 INPUT T
50 PRINT "DISCOUNT RATE";
60 INPUT D
69 REM - CONVERT PERCENT TO DECIMAL
70 D=D/100
80 PRINT "DAYS TO MATURITY";
90 INPUT N
99 REM - CALCULATE DISCOUNT, PRINT
100 D1=T*D*N/360
110 PRINT "DISCOUNT = $";D1
119 REM - CALCULATE COST, PRINT
120 PRINT "    COST = $";T-D1
129 REM - PRINT BLANK LINE TO SEPARATE DATA FROM QUESTION
130 PRINT
139 REM - RESTART OR END PROGRAM? USER INPUT REQUIRED
140 PRINT "MORE DATA? (1=YES, 0=NO)";
150 INPUT X
160 IF X=1 THEN 20
170 END
```

Principal on a Loan

This program calculates an initial amount borrowed. This amount is dependent upon the interest rate, the amount of regular payments, the number of payments per year, and the term of the loan.

The calculation is based on the formula:

$$P = \frac{R \cdot N}{i} \cdot \left(1 - \frac{1}{(1 + i/N)^{N \cdot Y}} \right)$$

where: P = principal
R = regular payment
i = annual interest rate
N = number of payments per year
Y = number of years

Example:

Susan has agreed to pay $250.00 bimonthly for 3 years to repay a loan with 20% interest. What is the amount of the loan?

Tom can afford to make payments of $180.00 per month to repay a loan. If he is willing to make payments for four and a half years and the loan company charges 16% interest, what is the maximum amount Tom can borrow?

```
PRINCIPAL ON A LOAN

REGULAR PAYMENT? 250
TERM IN YEARS? 3
ANNUAL INTEREST RATE? 20
# OF PAYMENTS PER YEAR? 6
PRINCIPAL = $3343.45

MORE DATA? (1=YES, 0=NO)? 1

REGULAR PAYMENT? 180
TERM IN YEARS? 4.5
ANNUAL INTEREST RATE? 16
# OF PAYMENTS PER YEAR? 12
PRINCIPAL = $6897.51

MORE DATA? (1=YES, 0=NO)? 0

5 GRAPHICS 0
10 PRINT "PRINCIPAL ON A LOAN"
20 PRINT
29 REM - STATEMENTS 30 TO 100 REQUEST USER INPUT
30 PRINT "REGULAR PAYMENT";
40 INPUT R
50 PRINT "TERM IN YEARS";
60 INPUT Y
70 PRINT "ANNUAL INTEREST RATE";
80 INPUT I
```

```
90 PRINT "# OF PAYMENTS PER YEAR";
100 INPUT N
108 REM - CALCULATE AMOUNT OF PRINCIPAL BY FORMULA;
109 REM - INTEREST CONVERTED FROM PERCENT TO  DECIMAL FOR CALCULATIONS
110 P=R*N*(1-1/((I/100)/N+1)^(N*Y))/(I/100)
119 REM - ROUND OFF TO NEAREST CENT, PRINT
120 PRINT "PRINCIPAL = $";
125 PRINT INT(P*100+0.5)/100
130 PRINT
139 REM - RESTART OR END PROGRAM?
140 PRINT "MORE DATA? (1=YES, 0=NO)";
150 INPUT X
160 IF X=1 THEN 20
170 END
```

OPTION

In some cases it may be more convenient to enter the term of the loan in years and months rather than years. The necessary program changes are listed following the example below.

Example:

What would be the amount of the mortgage if you were paying $75.00 a month for 11 months with 3% interest?

```
PRINCIPAL ON A LOAN

REGULAR PAYMENT? 75
TERM IN YEARS, MONTHS? 0,11
ANNUAL INTEREST RATE? 3
# OF PAYMENTS PER YEAR? 12
PRINCIPAL = $812.76

MORE DATA? (1=YES, 0=NO)? 0

1 REM - OPTION 50-65
5 GRAPHICS 0
10 PRINT "PRINCIPAL ON A LOAN"
    :
40 INPUT R
50 PRINT "TERM IN YEARS, MONTHS";
60 INPUT Y0,M
64 REM - CALCULATE YEARS FROM YEARS AND MONTHS
65 Y=(12*Y0+M)/12
70 PRINT "ANNUAL INTEREST RATE";
    :
170 END
```

Regular Payment on a Loan

This program calculates the amount required as regular payments in order to repay a loan over a specified time period. The specifications you must provide are the amount of the principal, the interest rate charged, the number of payments to be made per year, and the number of years to pay. This program assumes all installment payments will be equal.

The calculation is based on the formula:

$$R = \frac{i \cdot P/N}{1 - \left(\frac{i}{N} + 1\right) - N \cdot Y}$$

where: R = regular payment
i = annual interest rate
P = principal
N = number of payments per year
Y = number of years

Examples:

What must you pay on a loan of $4000.00 at 8% if payments are to be made quarterly for five years?

If Michael borrows $6500.00 at 12.5% from Best Rate Savings & Loan to be paid back over a period of five and a half years, what would his monthly payments be?

```
REGULAR PAYMENT ON A LOAN

TERM IN YEARS? 5
PRINCIPAL? 4000
ANNUAL INTEREST RATE? 8
# OF PAYMENTS PER YEAR? 4
REGULAR PAYMENT = $244.63

MORE DATA? (1=YES, 0=NO)? 1

TERM IN YEARS? 5.5
PRINCIPAL? 6500
ANNUAL INTEREST RATE? 12.5
# OF PAYMENTS PER YEAR? 12
REGULAR PAYMENT = $136.68

MORE DATA? (1=YES, 0=NO)? 0


5 GRAPHICS 0
10 PRINT "REGULAR PAYMENT ON A LOAN"
20 PRINT
29 REM - STATEMENTS 30 TO 100 REQUEST USER INPUT
30 PRINT "TERM IN YEARS";
40 INPUT Y
50 PRINT "PRINCIPAL";
60 INPUT P
```

```
70 PRINT "ANNUAL INTEREST RATE";
80 INPUT I
90 PRINT "# OF PAYMENTS PER YEAR";
100 INPUT N
108 REM - CALCULATE AMOUNT OF REGULAR PAYMENT BY FORMULA;
109 REM - INTEREST CONVERTED FROM PERCENT TO DECIMAL FOR CALCULATIONS
110 R=((I/100)*P/N)/(1-1/((I/100)/N+1)^(N*Y))
119 REM - ROUND OFF TO NEAREST CENT, PRINT
120 PRINT "REGULAR PAYMENT = $";
125 PRINT INT(R*100+0.5)/100
129 REM - PRINT BLANK LINE TO SEPARATE DATA FROM QUESTION
130 PRINT
139 REM - RESTART OR END PROGRAM? USER INPUT REQUIRED
140 PRINT "MORE DATA? (1=YES, 0=NO)";
150 INPUT X
160 IF X=1 THEN 20
170 END
```

OPTION

You may find it more convenient to enter the term of payment in years and months rather than years. The necessary program changes are listed following the example below.

Example:

Mr. Terry needs $10,000.00 to put down on a new home. Best Rate Savings & Loan offers this amount at 14.0% interest to be repaid over a period of 11 years and 5 months. What would be the amount of regular monthly payments?

```
REGULAR PAYMENT ON A LOAN

TERM IN YEARS, MONTHS? 11,5
PRINCIPAL? 10000
ANNUAL INTEREST RATE? 14
# OF PAYMENTS PER YEAR? 12
REGULAR PAYMENT = $146.59

MORE DATA? (1=YES, 0=NO)? 0

1 REM - OPTION 30-45
5 GRAPHICS 0
10 PRINT "REGULAR PAYMENT ON A LOAN"
  .
  .
29 REM - STATEMENTS 30 TO 100 REQUEST USER INPUT
30 PRINT "TERM IN YEARS, MONTHS";
40 INPUT YO,M
44 REM - CALCULATE YEARS FROM YEARS AND MONTHS
45 Y=(12*YO+M)/12
50 PRINT "PRINCIPAL";
  .
  .
170 END
```

Last Payment on a Loan

This program calculates the amount of the final payment on a loan. This final payment will complete amortization of a loan at the conclusion of its term. You must provide the amount of the loan, the amount of the regular payment, the interest rate charged, the number of payments per year, and the term of payment.

The amount of the last payment is normally different from the amount of the regular payment. The final payment will be a "balloon" payment if the final payment is larger than the regular payment. A balloon payment is necessary if applying the amount of the regular payment as the last payment leaves a remaining balance due. In order to entirely pay off the loan at the end of its term, this remaining balance is added to the amount of the regular payment to determine the amount of the last payment.

On the other hand, the amount of the final payment is sometimes less than the regular payment. If the regular payment as the last payment would result in a negative loan balance, then the last payment should be smaller. In this case the regular payment is adjusted by the amount of this hypothetical negative balance to determine the amount of the last payment.

$$\begin{matrix} \text{amount of} \\ \text{last payment} \end{matrix} = \begin{matrix} \text{regular} \\ \text{payment} \end{matrix} + \begin{matrix} \text{hypothetical balance due on a} \\ \text{loan after } N \cdot Y \text{ regular payments} \end{matrix}$$

where: N = number of payments per year
Y = number of years

Examples:

Lynn borrowed $6000.00 at 5% from her father for college expenses. If she pays $1000.00 annually for seven years, what will her last payment be?

Lynn borrows $1150.00 at 8% interest to be repaid at a rate of $75.00 per month. A year and two months later Lynn decides to go to Europe. How much must she pay next month to completely pay off her loan?

```
LAST PAYMENT ON A LOAN

REGULAR PAYMENT? 1000
PRINCIPAL? 6000
TERM IN YEARS? 7
ANNUAL INTEREST RATE? 5
# OF PAYMENTS PER YEAR? 1
LAST PAYMENT = $1300.59

MORE DATA? (1=YES, 0=NO)? 1

REGULAR PAYMENT? 75
PRINCIPAL? 1150
TERM IN YEARS? 1.17
ANNUAL INTEREST RATE? 8
# OF PAYMENTS PER YEAR? 12
LAST PAYMENT = $240.38

MORE DATA? (1=YES, 0=NO)? 0
```

```
5 GRAPHICS O
10 PRINT "LAST PAYMENT ON A LOAN"
20 PRINT
29 REM - STATEMENTS 30 TO 130 REQUEST USER INPUT
30 PRINT "REGULAR PAYMENT";
40 INPUT R
50 PRINT "PRINCIPAL";
60 INPUT P
70 PRINT "TERM IN YEARS";
80 INPUT Y
90 PRINT "ANNUAL INTEREST RATE";
100 INPUT I
109 REM - CONVERT INTEREST FROM PERCENT TO DECIMAL
110 I=I/100
120 PRINT "# OF PAYMENTS PER YEAR";
130 INPUT N
140 BO=P
149 REM - COMPUTE ALL PAYMENTS, BALANCES THROUGH LAST PAYMENT USING R
150 FOR J1=1 TO N*Y
159 REM - ROUND OFF INTEREST PAID TO NEAREST CENT
160 I1=INT((BO*I/N)*100+0.5)/100
169 REM - CALCULATE AMOUNT AMORTIZED WITH EACH PAYMENT
170 A=R-I1
179 REM - BALANCE REMAINING DECREASES WITH EACH PAYMENT
180 BO=BO-A
190 NEXT J1
199 REM - CALCULATE LAST PAYMENT, ROUND OFF, PRINT
200 PRINT "LAST PAYMENT = $";
205 PRINT INT((R+BO)*100+0.5)/100
210 PRINT
219 REM - RESTART OR END PROGRAM? USER INPUT REQUIRED
220 PRINT "MORE DATA? (1=YES, O=NO)";
230 INPUT X
240 IF X=1 THEN 20
250 END
```

OPTION

You may find it more convenient to enter the term of payment in years and months rather than years. The necessary program changes are listed following the example below.

Example:

If you pay $40.00 a month for two years and three months on a loan of $1200.00 at 7.5%, what amount will the last payment total?

```
LAST PAYMENT ON A LOAN

REGULAR PAYMENT? 40
PRINCIPAL? 1200
TERM IN YEARS, MONTHS? 2,3
```

```
ANNUAL INTEREST RATE? 7.5
# OF PAYMENTS PER YEAR? 12
LAST PAYMENT = $287.36

MORE DATA? (1=YES, 0=NO)? 0

1 REM - OPTION 70-85
5 GRAPHICS 0
10 PRINT "LAST PAYMENT ON A LOAN"
   .
   .
   .
60 INPUT P
70 PRINT "TERM IN YEARS, MONTHS";
80 INPUT YO,M
84 REM - CALCULATE YEARS FROM YEARS AND MONTHS
85 Y=(12*YO+M)/12
90 PRINT "ANNUAL INTEREST RATE";
   .
   .
   .
250 END
```

Remaining Balance on a Loan

This program calculates the balance remaining on a loan after a specified number of payments. It is necessary for you to provide the amount of the regular payment, the number of payments per year, the amount of the principal, the annual interest rate, and the payment number after which to calculate the remaining balance.

The remaining balance is calculated by the following method:

$$\begin{matrix} \text{remaining} \\ \text{balance} \end{matrix} = \text{principal} - \frac{\text{amount amortized after}}{N \cdot (Y-1) + N1 \text{ payments}}$$

where: N = number of payments per year
Y = year to calculate remaining balance
$N1$ = payment number in year Y to calculate remaining balance

Example:

Kelly has taken out a loan of $8000.00 at 17.2% interest. His regular payments are $200.00 per month. If he has paid through the tenth payment in the fourth year, how much more does Kelly owe on his loan?

```
REMAINING BALANCE ON A LOAN

REGULAR PAYMENT? 200
PRINCIPAL? 8000
# OF PAYMENTS PER YEAR? 12
ANNUAL INTEREST RATE? 17.2
LAST PAYMENT MADE:
(PAYMENT NUMBER,YEAR)? 10,4
REMAINING BALANCE = $2496.17

MORE DATA? (1=YES, 0=NO)? 0

5 GRAPHICS 0
10 PRINT "REMAINING BALANCE ON A LOAN"
20 PRINT
29 REM - STATEMENTS 30 TO 130 REQUEST USER INPUT
30 PRINT "REGULAR PAYMENT";
40 INPUT R
50 PRINT "PRINCIPAL";
60 INPUT P
70 PRINT "# OF PAYMENTS PER YEAR";
80 INPUT N
90 PRINT "ANNUAL INTEREST RATE";
100 INPUT I
109 REM - CONVERT FROM PERCENT TO DECIMAL
110 I=I/100
119 REM - ENTER THE PAYMENT NUMBER WITHIN THE YEAR, I.E. N1<=N
120 PRINT "LAST PAYMENT MADE:"
125 PRINT "(PAYMENT NUMBER,YEAR)";
130 INPUT N1,Y
```

```
139 REM - INITIALIZE REMAINING BALANCE
140 BO=P
149 REM - LOOP TO ACCUMULATE AMOUNT PAID SO FAR
150 FOR J1=1 TO N*(Y-1)+N1
159 REM - CALCULATE INTEREST PAID WITH EACH PAYMENT
160 I1=INT((BO*I/N)*100+0.5)/100
169 REM - CALCULATE AMOUNT AMORTIZED WITH EACH PAYMENT
170 A=R-I1
179 REM - CALCULATE REMAINING BALANCE ON PRINCIPAL
180 BO=BO-A
190 NEXT J1
199 REM - ROUND OFF, PRINT
200 PRINT "REMAINING BALANCE = $";
205 PRINT INT(BO*100+0.5)/100
210 PRINT
219 REM - RESTART OR END PROGRAM? USER INPUT REQUIRED
220 PRINT "MORE DATA? (1=YES, 0=NO)";
230 INPUT X
240 IF X=1 THEN 20
250 END
```

OPTION

You may wish to specify the number of the last payment made as the total payment number rather than the payment number within a certain year. For instance, when four payments are made per year, payment 3 of the third year would be entered as payment 11. The necessary program changes are listed following the example below.

Example:

John made ten quarterly payments of $550.00 on a loan of $6000.00 with 16% interest. What is his remaining balance?

```
REMAINING BALANCE ON A LOAN

REGULAR PAYMENT? 550
PRINCIPAL? 6000
# OF PAYMENTS PER YEAR? 4
ANNUAL INTEREST RATE? 16
NUMBER OF PAYMENTS MADE? 10
REMAINING BALANCE = $2278.09

MORE DATA? (1=YES, 0=NO)? 0


1 REM - OPTION 119-130, 150
5 GRAPHICS 0
10 PRINT "REMAINING BALANCE ON A LOAN"
  :
  :
110 I=I/100
```

```
119 REM - ENTER THE TOTAL NUMBER OF PAYMENTS MADE TO DATE
120 PRINT "NUMBER OF PAYMENTS MADE";
130 INPUT N1
139 REM - INITIALIZE REMAINING BALANCE
140 BO=P
149 REM - LOOP TO ACCUMULATE AMOUNT PAID SO FAR
150 FOR J1=1 TO N1
159 REM - CALCULATE INTEREST PAID WITH EACH PAYMENT
  :
250 END
```

Term of a Loan

This program calculates the period of time needed to repay a loan. You must specify the amount of the loan, the amount of the payments, the number of payments to be made per year, and the annual interest rate on the loan. All payments are assumed to be equal.

The term of payment is derived from the following formula:

$$Y = -\frac{\log\left(1 - \dfrac{P \cdot i}{N \cdot R}\right)}{\log\left(1 + \dfrac{i}{N}\right)} \cdot \frac{1}{N}$$

where: Y = term of payment in years
P = principal
i = annual interest rate
N = number of payments per year
R = amount of payments

Examples:

What would be the duration of payment on a mortgage of $20,000.00 at 18% when payments of $1000.00 are to be made quarterly?

Sally takes out a loan for $12,669.00 at 16.8%. Her payments are $512.34 every two months. What is the term of her loan?

```
TERM OF A LOAN

REGULAR PAYMENT? 1000
PRINCIPAL? 20000
ANNUAL INTEREST RATE? 18
# OF PAYMENTS PER YEAR? 4
TERM = 13.1 YEARS

MORE DATA? (1=YES, 0=NO)? 1

REGULAR PAYMENT? 512.34
PRINCIPAL? 12669
ANNUAL INTEREST RATE? 16.8
# OF PAYMENTS PER YEAR? 6
TERM = 7.1 YEARS

MORE DATA? (1=YES, 0=NO)? 0

5 GRAPHICS 0
10 PRINT "TERM OF A LOAN"
20 PRINT
29 REM - STATEMENTS 30 TO 100 REQUEST USER INPUT
30 PRINT "REGULAR PAYMENT";
40 INPUT R
50 PRINT "PRINCIPAL";
60 INPUT P
```

```
70 PRINT "ANNUAL INTEREST RATE";
80 INPUT I
90 PRINT "# OF PAYMENTS PER YEAR";
100 INPUT N
108 REM - CALCULATE TERM IN YEARS BY FORMULA;
109 REM - INTEREST CONVERTED FROM PERCENT TO DECIMAL FOR CALCULATION
110 Y=-(LOG(1-(P*(I/100))/(N*R))/(LOG(1+I/100/N)*N))
119 REM - ROUND OFF TO NEAREST TENTH, PRINT
120 PRINT "TERM = ";INT(Y*10+0.5)/10;
125 PRINT " YEARS"
130 PRINT
139 REM - RESTART OR END PROGRAM?
140 PRINT "MORE DATA? (1=YES, 0=NO)";
150 INPUT X
160 IF X=1 THEN 20
170 END
```

OPTION

It is possible to calculate the term of payment in years and months rather than just years. To do this, make the program changes listed following the example below.

Example:

Dick took out a loan for $8000.00 at 7.5%. Regular payments of $150.00 are to be made monthly. How long will it take to pay off the loan?

```
TERM OF A LOAN

REGULAR PAYMENT? 150
PRINCIPAL? 8000
ANNUAL INTEREST RATE? 7.5
# OF PAYMENTS PER YEAR? 12
TERM =5 YEARS,5 MONTHS

MORE DATA? (1=YES, 0=NO)? 0

1 REM - OPTION 114-120
5 GRAPHICS 0
10 PRINT "TERM OF A LOAN"
  :
110 Y=-(LOG(1-(P*(I/100))/(N*R))/(LOG(1+I/100/N)*N))
114 REM - CALCULATE YEARS AND MONTHS FROM YEARS
115 M=INT(Y*12+0.5)
116 YO=INT(M/12)
117 M=M-YO*12
119 REM - PRINT RESULTS
120 PRINT "TERM =";YO;" YEARS,";M;" MONTHS"
130 PRINT
  :
170 END
```

Annual Interest Rate on a Loan

This program calculates the rate at which interest is charged on a loan. To determine this rate you must enter the amount of the loan, the amount of the regular payment, the number of payments per year, and the term of the loan.

The annual interest rate is computed by the following method of approximation:

1. Guess an interest rate
   Initialize last guess to 0

2. Compute regular payment using guessed rate:

$$R_1 = \frac{i \cdot P/N}{1 - (1 + i/N)^{-N \cdot Y}}$$

   Round off R_1

3. If computed payment = actual payment, then current guess = approximate interest rate

4. Otherwise, save current guess and calculate a new guess:

$$i_2 = i$$
$$i = i \pm |(i - i_2)/2| \quad \begin{cases} + \text{ if } R_1 < R \\ - \text{ if } R_1 > R \end{cases}$$

5. Go to 2

   where: i = interest rate
   i_2 = previous interest rate
   R = input regular payment
   R_1 = computed regular payment
   P = principal
   N = number of payments per year
   Y = number of years

Examples:

Cindy borrowed $3000.00 from her friend George with an agreement to pay back $400.00 quarterly for two years. At what interest rate is she being charged?

To pay back a loan of $10,000.00 John contracted to make monthly payments of $120.00 for nine and a half years. At what rate is interest being charged?

```
ANNUAL INTEREST RATE ON A LOAN

REGULAR PAYMENT? 400
TERM IN YEARS? 2
PRINCIPAL? 3000
# OF PAYMENTS PER YEAR? 4
ANNUAL INTEREST RATE =5.827%

MORE DATA? (1=YES, 0=NO)? 1

REGULAR PAYMENT? 120
```

```
TERM IN YEARS? 9.5
PRINCIPAL? 10000
# OF PAYMENTS PER YEAR? 12
ANNUAL INTEREST RATE =6.933%

MORE DATA? (1=YES, 0=NO)? 0


5 GRAPHICS 0
10 PRINT "ANNUAL INTEREST RATE ON A LOAN"
20 PRINT
29 REM - STATEMENTS 30 TO 100 REQUEST USER INPUT
30 PRINT "REGULAR PAYMENT";
40 INPUT R
50 PRINT "TERM IN YEARS";
60 INPUT Y
70 PRINT "PRINCIPAL";
80 INPUT P
90 PRINT "# OF PAYMENTS PER YEAR";
100 INPUT N
109 REM - GUESS AN INTEREST RATE (10%) TO INITIATE TESTING
110 I=10
119 REM - I2=LAST GUESS OR ESTIMATE (START WITH 0)
120 I2=0
129 REM - COMPUTE REGULAR PAYMENT USING GUESSED INTEREST RATE
130 R1=(I*P/N)/(1-1/((I/N+1)^(N*Y)))
139 REM - ROUND OFF TO NEAREST CENT
140 R1=INT(R1*100+0.5)/100
149 REM - I3=NUMBER USED TO CLOSE IN ON INTEREST RATE
150 I3=ABS(I-I2)/2
159 REM - SAVE THIS GUESS
160 I2=I
168 REM - COMPARE COMPUTED PAYMENT (R1) TO INPUT PAYMENT (R);
169 REM - IF THEY'RE EQUAL, LAST RATE GUESSED=APPROXIMATE INTEREST RATE
170 IF R1=R THEN 230
180 IF R1>R THEN 210
189 REM - R1<R, RATE MUST BE HIGHER THAN LAST GUESS
190 I=I+I3
199 REM - RETEST WITH NEW GUESS
200 GOTO 130
209 REM - R1>R, RATE MUST BE LOWER THAN LAST GUESS
210 REM
212 I=I-I3
219 REM - RETEST WITH NEW GUESS
220 GOTO 130
229 REM - COMPUTE INTEREST TO PROPER PROPORTIONS, ROUND OFF,PRINT
230 I=((INT((I*1000)*100+0.5))/100)/1000
240 PRINT "ANNUAL INTEREST RATE =";
245 PRINT I*100;"%"
250 PRINT
259 REM - RESTART OR END PROGRAM? USER INPUT REQUIRED
260 PRINT "MORE DATA? (1=YES, 0=NO)";
270 INPUT X
280 IF X=1 THEN 20
290 END
```

OPTION

The above listing allows the term of the loan to be entered in years only. You may wish to enter the term in years and months rather than years. The necessary program changes are listed following the example below.

Example:

If Connie pays $100.00 per month for 11 years and 7 months on a $10,000.00 loan, what is the annual interest rate on the loan?

```
ANNUAL INTEREST RATE ON A LOAN

REGULAR PAYMENT? 100
TERM IN YEARS, MONTHS? 11,7
PRINCIPAL? 10000
# OF PAYMENTS PER YEAR? 12
ANNUAL INTEREST RATE =6.002%

MORE DATA? (1=YES, 0=NO)? 0

1 REM - OPTION 50-65
5 GRAPHICS 0
10 PRINT "ANNUAL INTEREST RATE ON A LOAN"
  :
40 INPUT R
50 PRINT "TERM IN YEARS, MONTHS";
60 INPUT YO,M
64 REM - CALCULATE YEARS FROM YEARS AND MONTHS
65 Y=(12*YO+M)/12
70 PRINT "PRINCIPAL";
  :
290 END
```

Mortgage Amortization Table

This program calculates and prints a loan repayment schedule. This schedule provides the following outputs:

1. Payment number
2. Amount of each payment paid as interest
3. Amount of the loan amortized with each payment
4. Balance remaining on the principal at the time of each payment
5. Accumulated interest paid at the time of each payment
6. Amount of the last payment

In addition, the yearly totals of interest paid and amount amortized are tabulated and printed.

To use this program you must supply the amount of the regular payment, the term of payment, the number of payments per year, the amount of the principal and the annual interest rate.

The schedule is calculated in the following manner:

1. Payment number = payment number within each year
2. Amount of each payment paid as interest = remaining balance $\cdot i/N$
   where: i = annual interest rate
   N = number of payments per year
3. Amount amortized with each payment = $R - I$
   where: R = amount of regular payment
   I = amount of each payment paid as interest
4. Balance remaining = $P - \Sigma A$
   where: P = principal
   ΣA = sum of amounts amortized with each payment to date
5. Accumulated interest = I
   where: ΣI = sum of amounts of each payment paid as interest to date
6. Amount of last payment = $R + (P - R \cdot N \cdot Y)$
   where: R = regular payment
   P = principal
   N = number of payments per year
   Y = number of years

Example:

David needs $2100.00 to pay off some debts. His sister offers him the money at 6% interest. With payments of $75.00 monthly for two and a half years, what is David's repayment schedule?

```
MORTGAGE AMORTIZATION TABLE

REGULAR PAYMENT? 75
TERM IN YEARS? 2.5
PRINCIPAL? 2100
ANNUAL INTEREST RATE? 6
```

PAYMENTS PER YEAR? 12
START WITH WHAT YEAR? 1

PRESS 'RETURN' TO CONTINUE?

MORTGAGE AMORTIZATION TABLE

PRINCIPAL $2100 AT 6% FOR 2.5 YEARS
REGULAR PAYMENT = $75

NO.	INTR.	AMORT.	BALANCE	ACCUM.INT.
1	10.5	64.5	2035.5	10.5
2	10.18	64.82	1970.68	20.68
3	9.85	65.15	1905.53	30.53
4	9.53	65.47	1840.06	40.06
5	9.2	65.8	1774.26	49.26
6	8.87	66.13	1708.13	58.13
7	8.54	66.46	1641.67	66.67
8	8.21	66.79	1574.88	74.88
9	7.87	67.13	1507.75	82.75
10	7.54	67.46	1440.29	90.29
11	7.2	67.8	1372.49	97.49
12	6.86	68.14	1304.35	104.35

YR. 1: INTEREST = $104.35
       AMORTIZED = $795.65

PRESS 'RETURN' TO CONTINUE?

MORTGAGE AMORTIZATION TABLE

PRINCIPAL $2100 AT 6% FOR 2.5 YEARS
REGULAR PAYMENT = $75

NO.	INTR.	AMORT.	BALANCE	ACCUM.INT.
1	6.52	68.48	1235.87	110.87
2	6.18	68.82	1167.05	117.05
3	5.84	69.16	1097.89	122.89
4	5.49	69.51	1028.38	128.38
5	5.14	69.86	958.52	133.52
6	4.79	70.21	888.31	138.31
7	4.44	70.56	817.75	142.75
8	4.09	70.91	746.84	146.84
9	3.73	71.27	675.57	150.57
10	3.38	71.62	603.95	153.95
11	3.02	71.98	531.97	156.97
12	2.66	72.34	459.63	159.63

YR. 2: INTEREST = $55.28
       AMORTIZED = $844.72

PRESS 'RETURN' TO CONTINUE?

MORTGAGE AMORTIZATION TABLE

```
PRINCIPAL $2100 AT 6% FOR 2.5 YEARS
REGULAR PAYMENT = $75
```

NO.	INTR.	AMORT.	BALANCE	ACCUM.INT.
1	2.3	72.7	386.93	161.93
2	1.93	73.07	313.86	163.86
3	1.57	73.43	240.43	165.43
4	1.2	73.8	166.63	166.63
5	0.83	74.17	92.46	167.46
6	0.46	92.46	0	167.92

```
    LAST PAYMENT = $92.92
YR. 3: INTEREST = $8.29
       AMORTIZED = $459.63


CHANGE DATA AND RECOMPUTE?
(1=YES, 0=NO)? 0
```

```
5 GRAPHICS 0
6 DIM W$(1)
10 PRINT "MORTGAGE AMORTIZATION TABLE"
20 PRINT
29 REM - STATEMENTS 30 TO 150 REQUEST USER INPUT
30 PRINT "REGULAR PAYMENT";
40 INPUT R
50 PRINT "TERM IN YEARS";
60 INPUT Y
70 PRINT "PRINCIPAL";
80 INPUT P
90 PRINT "ANNUAL INTEREST RATE";
100 INPUT I
109 REM - CONVERT FROM PERCENT TO DECIMAL
110 I=I/100
120 PRINT "PAYMENTS PER YEAR";
130 INPUT N
140 PRINT "START WITH WHAT YEAR";
150 INPUT X
159 REM - START PRINTING AT BEGINNING OF A YEAR
160 X=INT(X)
169 REM - INITIALIZE VARIABLES
170 C1=0
180 I2=0
190 I3=0
200 J0=0
210 N1=N
220 K=20
230 B0=P
240 A1=0
250 A2=0
259 REM - TERM LESS THAN ONE YEAR?
260 IF INT(Y)>=1 THEN 270
262 N1=((Y-INT(Y))*12)/12*N
264 J0=J0+1
265 GOTO 280
269 REM - LOOP FOR EACH YEAR
270 FOR J0=1 TO INT(Y)
```

```
279 REM - START PRINTING?
280 IF JO<X THEN 410
289 REM - CHECK FOR FULL SCREEN (20 LINES)
290 IF K+N+3<20 THEN 400
295 REM - WAIT FOR OPERATOR CUE TO GO TO NEXT SCREEN
297 PRINT
300 PRINT "PRESS 'RETURN' TO CONTINUE";
310 INPUT W$
330 PRINT
339 REM - PRINT PAGE HEADINGS
340 GRAPHICS 0
342 POSITION 0,23
345 PRINT "MORTGAGE AMORTIZATION TABLE"
346 PRINT
350 PRINT "PRINCIPAL $";P;" AT ";I*100;
355 PRINT "% FOR ";Y;" YEARS"
360 PRINT "REGULAR PAYMENT = $";R
370 PRINT
380 PRINT "NO. INTR. AMORT.   ";
385 PRINT "BALANCE    ACCUM.INT."
389 REM - COUNT LINES PRINTED ON EACH PAGE IN K
390 K=7
400 K=K+N+3
410 FOR J1=1 TO N1
419 REM - CALCULATE INTEREST PAID THIS PAYMENT, ROUND OFF
420 I1=INT((BO*I/N)*100+0.5)/100
429 REM - COUNT NUMBER OF PAYMENTS MADE SO FAR
430 C1=C1+1
439 REM - CALCULATE AMOUNT AMORTIZED THIS PAYMENT
440 A=R-I1
449 REM - SUM AMOUNT AMORTIZED TO DATE
450 A1=A1+A
460 BO=P-A1
468 REM - LAST PAYMENT? IF YES, CALCULATE AMOUNT SO THAT THE
469 REM - BALANCE DUE EQUALS $00.00 AFTER THIS PAYMENT
470 IF C1<>N*Y THEN 520
475 REM - CALCULATE BALANCE DUE
480 R=R+BO
490 A=A+BO
500 A1=A1+BO
510 BO=0
519 REM - SUM INTEREST PAID TO DATE
520 I2=I2+I1
529 REM - SUM INTEREST PAID THIS YEAR
530 I3=I3+I1
539 REM - SUM AMOUNT AMORTIZED THIS YEAR
540 A2=A2+A
541 A2=INT(A2*100+0.5)/100
549 REM - STARTED PRINTING? IF YES, PRINT COMPUTED VALUES IN TABLE
550 IF JO<X THEN 570
551 A=INT(A*100+0.5)/100
560 PRINT J1;
561 POSITION 6,23
562 PRINT I1;
563 POSITION 12,23
```

```
564 PRINT A;
565 BO=INT(BO*100+0.5)/100
566 POSITION 20,23
567 PRINT BO;
568 POSITION 30,23
569 PRINT I2
570 NEXT J1
579 REM - LAST PAYMENT? IF YES, ROUND OFF, PRINT
580 IF C1<>N*Y THEN 600
590 PRINT "    LAST PAYMENT = $";INT(R*100+0.5)/100
599 REM - STARTED PRINTING? IF YES,PRINT YEARLY TOTALS
600 IF JO<X THEN 640
610 PRINT
620 PRINT "YR. ";JO;": INTEREST = $";I3
625 PRINT "        AMORTIZED = $";A2
630 PRINT
639 REM - COMPLETED TERM?
640 IF JO>Y THEN 720
649 REM - REINITIALIZE YEARLY VARIABLES
650 I3=0
660 A2=0
670 NEXT JO
671 JO=JO-1
679 REM - NEED TO PRINT A PARTIAL YEAR?
680 IF Y<>JO THEN 262
720 PRINT
729 REM - RESTART OR END PROGRAM? USER INPUT REQUIRED
730 PRINT "CHANGE DATA AND RECOMPUTE?"
735 PRINT "(1=YES, 0=NO)";
740 INPUT Z
750 IF Z=1 THEN 20
760 END
```

OPTION

You may wish to enter the term of payment in years and months rather than years. The necessary program changes are listed following the example below.

Example:

If you took out a loan for $700.00 from a friend at 9% interest and were to pay $100.00 per month for eight months, what would your repayment schedule be?

```
MORTGAGE AMORTIZATION TABLE

REGULAR PAYMENT? 100
TERM IN YEARS, MONTHS? 0,8
PRINCIPAL? 700
ANNUAL INTEREST RATE? 9
```

```
PAYMENTS PER YEAR? 12
START WITH WHAT YEAR? 1

PRESS 'RETURN' TO CONTINUE?

MORTGAGE AMORTIZATION TABLE

PRINCIPAL $700 AT 9% FOR 0 YEARS AND 8 MONTHS
REGULAR PAYMENT = $100

NO.          INTR.        AMORT.       BALANCE      ACCUM.INT.
1            5.25         94.75        605.25       5.25
2            4.54         95.46        509.79       9.79
3            3.82         96.18        413.61       13.61
4            3.1          96.9         316.71       16.71
5            2.38         97.62        219.09       19.09
6            1.64         98.36        120.73       20.73
7            0.91         99.09        21.64        21.64
YR. 1: INTEREST = $21.64
       AMORTIZED = $678.36


CHANGE DATA AND RECOMPUTE?
(1=YES, 0=NO)? 0

1 REM - OPTION 50-65, 355
10 PRINT "MORTGAGE AMORTIZATION TABLE"
40 INPUT R
50 PRINT "TERM IN YEARS, MONTHS";
60 INPUT Y0,M
64 REM - CONVERT YEARS AND MONTHS TO YEARS
65 Y=(12*Y0+M)/12
70 PRINT "PRINCIPAL";
   .
   .
345 PRINT "MORTGAGE AMORTIZATION TABLE"
346 PRINT
350 PRINT "PRINCIPAL $";P;" AT ";I*100;
355 PRINT "% FOR ";Y0;" YEARS AND ";M;" MONTHS"
360 PRINT "REGULAR PAYMENT = $";R
   .
   .
760 END
```

Greatest Common Denominator

This program calculates the greatest common denominator of two integers. It is based on the Euclidean algorithm for finding the GCD:

1. Enter A, B
   A = absolute value of A
   B = absolute value of B

2. Calculate $R = A - B \cdot$ (integer of (A/B))

3. Is $R = 0$? If yes, the GCD $= B$
   If no, go to step 4

4. $A = B$
   $B = R$

5. Go to step 2

Example:

Find the greatest common denominator of 50 and 18, 115 and 150.

```
GREATEST COMMON DENOMINATOR

(ENTER 0,0 TO END PROGRAM)
ENTER TWO NUMBERS? 50,18
G.C.D:2

ENTER TWO NUMBERS? 115,150
G.C.D:5

ENTER TWO NUMBERS? 0,0

5 GRAPHICS 0
10 PRINT "GREATEST COMMON DENOMINATOR"
20 PRINT
30 PRINT "(ENTER 0,0 TO END PROGRAM)"
40 PRINT "ENTER TWO NUMBERS";
50 INPUT A,B
59 REM - END PROGRAM?
60 IF A<>0 THEN 90
70 IF B<>0 THEN 90
80 GOTO 190
89 REM - CALCULATE GCD ACCORDING TO EUCLIDEAN ALGORITHM, PRINT RESULT
90 A=ABS(A)
100 B=ABS(B)
110 R=A-B*INT(A/B)
120 IF R=0 THEN 160
130 A=B
140 B=R
150 GOTO 110
```

```
160 PRINT "G.C.D:";B
169 REM - PRINT BLANK LINE TO SEPARATE SETS OF DATA
170 PRINT
179 REM -RESTART PROGRAM
180 GOTO 40
190 END
```

Prime Factors of Integers

This program lists the prime factors of an integer. It will not test for the integer 0.

Examples:

What are the prime factors of −49?
   Factor 92 into primes.

```
PRIME FACTORS OF INTEGERS

(ENTER 0 TO END PROGRAM)
NUMBER? -49
-1
7^2

NUMBER? 92
1
2^2
23^1

NUMBER? 0

5 GRAPHICS 0
10 PRINT "PRIME FACTORS OF INTEGERS"
20 PRINT
30 PRINT "(ENTER 0 TO END PROGRAM)"
40 PRINT "NUMBER";
50 INPUT Z
59 REM - END PROGRAM?
60 IF Z=0 THEN 200
69 REM - THE SIGN OF THE NUMBER IS ALWAYS A FACTOR
70 PRINT SGN(Z)
79 REM - USE ABSOLUTE VALUE FOR CALCULATIONS
80 Z=ABS(Z)
88 REM - LOOP TO TEST ALL INTEGERS (2 THROUGH Z) AS PRIME FACTORS
89 REM - INTEGERS Z/2 THROUGH Z WILL HAVE NO NEW FACTORS
90 FOR I=2 TO Z/2
100 S=0
110 IF Z/I<>INT(Z/I) THEN 150
120 Z=Z/I
130 S=S+1
140 GOTO 110
149 REM - FIND A PRIME FACTOR? IF YES, PRINT
150 IF S=0 THEN 170
159 REM - PRINT FACTORS WITH EXPONENTS; I^S=I TO THE S POWER
160 PRINT I;"^";S
170 NEXT I
180 PRINT
190 GOTO 40
200 END
```

Area of a Polygon

This program calculates the area of a polygon. You must supply the x and y coordinates of all vertices. Coordinates must be entered in order of successive vertices.

The formula used to calculate the area is:

$$\text{Area} = [(x_1 + x_2) \cdot (y_1 - y_2) + (x_2 + x_3) \cdot (y_2 - y_3) + \ldots (x_n + x_1) \cdot (y_n - y_1)]/2$$

where n = the number of vertices

The number of vertices you may enter is currently limited to 24. You may increase or decrease this limit by altering statement 30 according to the following scheme:

30 DIM X($N+1$), Y($N+1$)

Example:

Approximate the area of Lake Boyer.

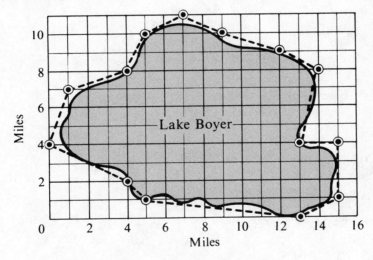

```
AREA OF A POLYGON

(ENTER 0 TO END)
NUMBER OF VERTICES? 14
COORDINATES:
            VERTEX 1? 0,4
                   2? 1,7
                   3? 4,8
                   4? 5,10
                   5? 7,11
                   6? 9,10
                   7? 12,9
                   8? 14,8
                   9? 13,4
                   10? 15,4
                   11? 15,1
```

```
                              12? 13,0
                              13? 5,1
                              14? 4,2
AREA = 108
(ENTER O TO END)
NUMBER OF VERTICES? O

5 GRAPHICS O
10 PRINT "AREA OF A POLYGON"
20 PRINT
29 REM - COORDINATE ARRAYS SHOULD BE SET TO (NUMBER OF VERTICES +1)
30 DIM X(25),Y(25)
40 PRINT "(ENTER O TO END)"
45 PRINT "NUMBER OF VERTICES";
50 INPUT N
59 REM - END PROGRAM?
60 IF N=O THEN 230
69 REM - LOOP TO ENTER COORDINATES IN ORDER OF SUCCESSIVE VERTICES
70 FOR I=1 TO N
80 IF I>1 THEN 110
90 PRINT "COORDINATES:"
95 PRINT "                    VERTEX ";I;
100 GOTO 120
110 PRINT "                          ";I;
120 INPUT X1,Y1
122 X(I)=X1
124 Y(I)=Y1
130 NEXT I
139 REM - FIRST VERTEX SERVES AS LAST VERTEX
140 X(N+1)=X(1)
150 Y(N+1)=Y(1)
160 A=0
169 REM - CALCULATE AREA, PRINT
170 FOR I=1 TO N
180 A=A+(X(I)+X(I+1))*(Y(I)-Y(I+1))
190 NEXT I
200 PRINT "AREA = ";ABS(A)/2
210 PRINT
219 REM - RESTART PROGRAM
220 GOTO 40
230 END
```

Parts of a Triangle

This program calculates three unknown parts of a triangle when three parts are given. At least one part given must be the length of a side. There are five possibilities for data entry:

1. Angle, side, angle
2. Side, angle, side
3. Angle, angle, side
4. Side, side, angle
5. Side, side, side

Data must be entered in the order it appears in a triangle, either clockwise or counterclockwise.

Example:

The base of a triangle measures 14 inches. The base angles measure 0.45 and 2.1 radians. What are the measurements of the triangle?

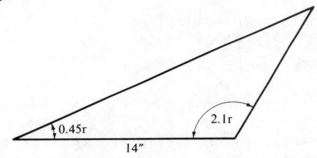

```
PARTS OF A TRIANGLE

PROBLEM TYPES:
                1=ASA,  2=SAS,  3=AAS
                4=SSA,  5=SSS,  6=END

ENTER PROBLEM TYPE? 1
ENTER ANGLE, SIDE, ANGLE? 0.45,14,2.1

SIDE 1 = 10.919
OPPOSITE ANGLE = 0.45 RADIANS
SIDE 2 = 21.67
OPPOSITE ANGLE = 2.1 RADIANS
SIDE 3 = 14
OPPOSITE ANGLE = 0.592 RADIANS

ENTER PROBLEM TYPE? 6

5 GRAPHICS 0
10 PRINT "PARTS OF A TRIANGLE"
20 PRINT
```

```
30 DIM A(3),S(3)
35 PI=3.1415927
38 REM - ENTER NUMBER OF PROBLEM TYPE ACCORDING TO KNOWN PARTS
39 REM - OF THE TRIANGLE WHERE A=ANGLE, S=LENGTH OF SIDE
40 PRINT "PROBLEM TYPES:"
50 PRINT "                     1=ASA, 2=SAS, 3=AAS"
55 PRINT "                     4=SSA, 5=SSS, 6=END"
57 PRINT
60 PRINT "ENTER PROBLEM TYPE";
70 INPUT X
79 REM - DIRECT PROGRAM TO PROPER CALCULATIONS
80 IF X=6 THEN 560
90 IF X=5 THEN 390
100 IF X=4 THEN 300
110 IF X=3 THEN 260
120 IF X=2 THEN 190
125 IF X<>1 THEN 40
130 PRINT "ENTER ANGLE, SIDE, ANGLE";
140 INPUT A1,S3,A2
141 A(1)=A1
142 S(3)=S3
143 A(2)=A2
150 A(3)=PI-A(1)-A(2)
160 S(1)=S(3)*SIN(A(1))/SIN(A(3))
170 S(2)=S(3)*SIN(A(2))/SIN(A(3))
180 GOTO 440
190 PRINT "ENTER SIDE, ANGLE, SIDE";
200 INPUT S3,A1,S2
201 S(3)=S3
202 A(1)=A1
203 S(2)=S2
210 S(1)=SQR(S(3)^2+S(2)^2-2*S(3)*S(2)*COS(A(1)))
220 A(2)=SIN(A(1))/S(1)*S(2)
230 A(2)=ATN(A(2)/SQR(1-(A(2))^2))
240 A(3)=PI-A(1)-A(2)
250 GOTO 440
260 PRINT "ENTER ANGLE, ANGLE, SIDE";
270 INPUT A3,A2,S3
271 A(3)=A3
272 A(2)=A2
273 S(3)=S3
280 A(1)=PI-A(2)-A(3)
290 GOTO 160
300 PRINT "ENTER SIDE, SIDE, ANGLE";
310 INPUT S1,S2,A1
311 S(1)=S1
312 S(2)=S2
313 A(1)=A1
320 T=S(2)*SIN(A(1))
330 IF S(1)<T THEN 520
340 S(3)=SQR(S(2)^2-T^2)
350 IF S(1)<=T THEN 380
360 Y=SQR(S(1)^2-T^2)
370 S(3)=S(3)+Y
380 GOTO 220
```

```
390 PRINT "ENTER SIDE, SIDE, SIDE";
400 INPUT S1,S2,S3
401 S(1)=S1
402 S(2)=S2
403 S(3)=S3
410 A(1)=(S(2)^2+S(3)^2-S(1)^2)/2/S(2)/S(3)
420 A(1)=ATN((SQR(1-(A(1))^2))/A(1))
430 GOTO 220
440 PRINT
449 REM - RESTART PROGRAM
450 FOR I=1 TO 3
459 REM - THE ANGLE OF A TRIANGLE CANNOT BE LESS THAN ZERO
460 IF A(I)<0 THEN 520
470 PRINT "SIDE ";I;" = ";
475 PRINT INT(S(I)*1000+0.5)/1000
480 PRINT "OPPOSITE ANGLE = ";
485 PRINT INT(A(I)*1000+0.5)/1000;
486 PRINT " RADIANS"
490 NEXT I
500 PRINT
510 GOTO 60
520 PRINT
530 PRINT "NO SOLUTION"
540 PRINT
549 REM - RESTART PROGRAM
550 GOTO 60
560 END
```

OPTION

It may be more convenient for you to work with angles in degrees rather than radians. The necessary program changes are listed following the examples below.

Examples:

A square measures 8.76 by 8.76 inches. What is the length of its diagonal?

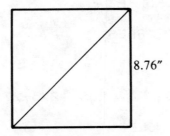

8.76″

The ladder of a slide measures 10 feet, the slide measures 14 feet, and it covers 13 feet of ground from base of ladder to tip of slide. How steep is the slide?

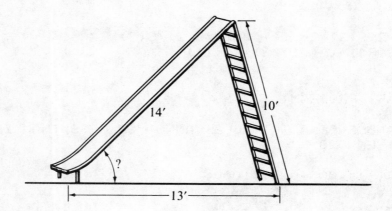

```
PARTS OF A TRIANGLE

PROBLEM TYPES:
                    1=ASA,  2=SAS,  3=AAS
                    4=SSA,  5=SSS,  6=END

ENTER PROBLEM TYPE? 2
ENTER SIDE, ANGLE, SIDE? 8.76,90,8.76

SIDE 1 = 12.389
OPPOSITE ANGLE = 90 DEGREES
SIDE 2 = 8.76
OPPOSITE ANGLE = 45 DEGREES
SIDE 3 = 8.76
OPPOSITE ANGLE = 45 DEGREES

ENTER PROBLEM TYPE? 5
ENTER SIDE, SIDE, SIDE? 10,13,14

SIDE 1 = 10
OPPOSITE ANGLE = 43.279 DEGREES
SIDE 2 = 13
OPPOSITE ANGLE = 63.027 DEGREES
SIDE 3 = 14
OPPOSITE ANGLE = 73.694 DEGREES

ENTER PROBLEM TYPE? 6

1 REM - OPTION 36-37, 145-146, 205, 275-276, 315, 485-486
5 GRAPHICS 0
10 PRINT "PARTS OF A TRIANGLE"
  .
  .
35 PI=3.1415927
36 REM - SET CONVERSION FACTOR FOR CONVERTING DEGREES TO RADIANS
37 C=0.0174532927
```

```
38 REM - ENTER NUMBER OF PROBLEM TYPE ACCORDING TO KNOWN PARTS
    .
    .
143 A(2)=A2
145 A(1)=A(1)*C
146 A(2)=A(2)*C
150 A(3)=PI-A(1)-A(2)
    .
    .
203 S(2)=S2
205 A(1)=A(1)*C
210 S(1)=SQR(S(3)^2+S(2)^2-2*S(3)*S(2)*COS(A(1)))
    .
    .
273 S(3)=S3
275 A(3)=A(3)*C
276 A(2)=A(2)*C
280 A(1)=PI-A(2)-A(3)
    .
    .
313 A(1)=A1
315 A(1)=A(1)*C
320 T=S(2)*SIN(A(1))
    .
    .
480 PRINT "OPPOSITE ANGLE = ";
485 PRINT INT(A(I)/C*1000+0.5)/1000;
486 PRINT " DEGREES"
490 NEXT I
    .
    .
560 END
```

Analysis of Two Vectors

This program calculates the angle between two given vectors, the angle between each vector and axis, and the magnitude of each vector. The vectors are given in three-dimensional space.

Example:

Find the angle (θ) between a diagonal of a cube and a diagonal of one of its faces. The cube measures $4 \times 4 \times 4$.

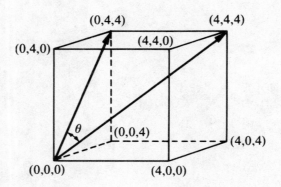

```
ANALYSIS OF TWO VECTORS

VECTOR 1: X,Y,Z? 0,4,4
VECTOR 2: X,Y,Z? 4,4,4

VECTOR 1 :
MAGNITUDE: 5.65685417
ANGLE WITH X-AXIS: 90.000002
ANGLE WITH Y-AXIS: 44.99999996
ANGLE WITH Z-AXIS: 44.99999996

VECTOR 2 :
MAGNITUDE: 6.92820314
ANGLE WITH X-AXIS: 54.73561062
ANGLE WITH Y-AXIS: 54.73561062
ANGLE WITH Z-AXIS: 54.73561062

ANGLE BETWEEN VECTORS: 35.26438793

MORE DATA (1=YES, 0=NO)? 0

5 GRAPHICS 0
10 PRINT "ANALYSIS OF TWO VECTORS"
20 PRINT
30 DIM X(2),Y(2),Z(2),M(2)
35 PI=3.1415927
```

```
39 REM - STATEMENTS 40 TO 70 REQUEST USER INPUT
40 PRINT "VECTOR 1: X,Y,Z";
50 INPUT X1,Y1,Z1
51 X(1)=X1
52 Y(1)=Y1
53 Z(1)=Z1
60 60 PRINT "VECTOR 2: X,Y,Z";
70 INPUT X2,Y2,Z2
71 X(2)=X2
72 Y(2)=Y2
73 Z(2)=Z2
80 PRINT
89 REM - LOOP TO ANALYZE BOTH VECTORS
90 FOR I=1 TO 2
99 REM - CALCULATE MAGNITUDE, PRINT
100 M(I)=SQR(X(I)^2+Y(I)^2+Z(I)^2)
109 REM - IF VECTOR A POINT? IF YES, CANNOT COMPUTE AN ANGLE
110 IF M(I)=0 THEN 220
120 PRINT "VECTOR ";I;" :"
130 PRINT "MAGNITUDE: ";M(I)
139 REM - CONVERSION FACTOR FOR RADIANS TO DEGREES
140 S=57.29578
149 REM - CALCULATE ANGLE BETWEEN VECTOR AND X-AXIS, PRINT
150 J=X(I)/M(I)
160 PRINT "ANGLE WITH X-AXIS: ";
162 IF J=0 THEN 167
165 PRINT ATN((SQR(1-J^2))/J)*S
166 GOTO 170
167 PRINT S*PI/2
169 REM - CALCULATE ANGLE BETWEEN VECTOR AND Y-AXIS, PRINT
170 J=Y(I)/M(I)
180 PRINT "ANGLE WITH Y-AXIS: ";
182 IF J=0 THEN 187
185 PRINT ATN((SQR(1-J^2))/J)*S
186 GOTO 190
187 PRINT S*PI/2
189 REM - CALCULATE ANGLE BETWEEN VECTOR AND Z-AXIS, PRINT
190 J=Z(I)/M(I)
200 PRINT "ANGLE WITH Z-AXIS: ";
202 IF J=0 THEN 207
205 PRINT ATN((SQR(1-J^2))/J)*S
206 GOTO 210
207 PRINT S*PI/2
210 PRINT
220 NEXT I
230 J=0
239 REM - IF EITHER VECTOR A POINT, CANNOT COMPUTE ANGLE
240 IF M(1)=0 THEN 310
250 IF M(2)=0 THEN 310
259 REM - CALCULATE ANGLE BETWEEN VECTORS
260 J=(X(1)*X(2)+Y(1)*Y(2)+Z(1)*Z(2))/M(1)/M(2)
269 REM - ARE THE VECTORS PERPENDICULAR?
270 IF J<>0 THEN 300
280 J=90
290 GOTO 310
```

```
299 REM - CALCULATE ANGLE IN DEGREES, PRINT
300 J=ATN(SQR(1-J^2)/J)*S
310 PRINT "ANGLE BETWEEN VECTORS: ";J
320 PRINT
329 REM - RESTART OR END PROGRAM?
330 PRINT "MORE DATA (1=YES, 0=NO)";
340 INPUT Z
350 IF Z=1 THEN 40
360 END
```

Operations on Two Vectors

This program performs four operations on two vectors given in three-dimensional space. The operations performed are:

1. Addition
2. Subtraction
3. Scalar (dot) product
4. Cross product

Example:

Vectors are drawn from the origin to two points $A(5,-1,2)$ and $B(1,4,9)$. Add, subtract, and find the dot and cross product of these vectors.

```
OPERATIONS ON TWO VECTORS

VECTOR A: X,Y,Z? 5,-1,2
VECTOR B: X,Y,Z? 1,4,9

A+B = 6,3,11
A-B = 4,-5,-7
A.B = 19
A*B = -17,-43,21

MORE DATA (1=YES, 0=NO)? 0

5 GRAPHICS 0
10 PRINT "OPERATIONS ON TWO VECTORS"
20 PRINT
30 PRINT "VECTOR A: X,Y,Z";
40 INPUT X1,Y1,Z1
50 PRINT "VECTOR B: X,Y,Z";
60 INPUT X2,Y2,Z2
70 PRINT
79 REM - PERFORM VECTOR ADDITION, PRINT RESULTING VECTOR COORDINATES
80 PRINT "A+B = ";X1+X2;",";Y1+Y2;
85 PRINT ",";Z1+Z2
89 REM - PERFORM VECTOR SUBTRACTION, PRINT RESULTING VECTOR COORDINATES
90 PRINT "A-B = ";X1-X2;",";Y1-Y2;
95 PRINT ",";Z1-Z2
99 REM - CALCULATE DOT PRODUCT, PRINT
100 PRINT "A.B = ";X1*X2+Y1*Y2+Z1*Z2
109 REM - CALCULATE CROSS PRODUCT, PRINT RESULTING VECTOR COORDINATES
110 PRINT "A*B = ";Y1*Z2-Z1*Y2;",";
115 PRINT Z1*X2-X1*Z2;",";X1*Y2-Y1*X2
120 PRINT
129 REM - RESTART OR END PROGRAM?
130 PRINT "MORE DATA (1=YES, 0=NO)";
140 INPUT Z
150 IF Z=1 THEN 20
160 END
```

Angle Conversion: Radians to Degrees

This program converts an angle given in radians to degrees, minutes, and seconds.

Example:

How many degrees, minutes, and seconds are there in an angle of 2.5 radians? In 118 radians?

```
ANGLE CONVERSION: RADIANS TO DEGREES

(ENTER 0 TO END THIS PROGRAM)
ANGLE IN RADIANS? 2.5

   DEGREES = 143
   MINUTES = 14
   SECONDS = 22.01

ANGLE IN RADIANS? 118

   DEGREES = 280
   MINUTES = 54
   SECONDS = 6.77

ANGLE IN RADIANS? 0
```

```
5 GRAPHICS 0
6 PI=3.1415927
10 PRINT "ANGLE CONVERSION: RADIANS TO DEGREES"
20 PRINT
30 PRINT "(ENTER 0 TO END THIS PROGRAM)"
50 PRINT "ANGLE IN RADIANS";
60 INPUT R
69 REM - TEST FOR END OF PROGRAM
70 IF R=0 THEN 170
79 REM - CONVERT RADIANS TO SECONDS
80 A=3600*180*R/PI
89 REM - CALCULATE NUMBER OF WHOLE DEGREES
90 D=INT(A/3600)
99 REM - CALCULATE NUMBER OF FULL CIRCLES
100 D1=INT(D/360)
105 PRINT
109 REM - CALCULATE DEGREES OF ANGLE WITHIN 360 DEGREES, PRINT
110 PRINT "   DEGREES = ";D-360*D1
119 REM - CALCULATE MINUTES, PRINT
120 PRINT "   MINUTES = ";
125 PRINT INT((A-D*3600)/60)
129 REM - CALCULATE SECONDS, ROUND OFF, PRINT
130 S=A-D*3600-(INT((A-D*3600)/60))*60
140 PRINT "   SECONDS = ";
145 PRINT INT(100*S+0.5)/100
```

```
150 PRINT
159 REM - RESTART PROGRAM
160 GOTO 50
170 END
```

OPTION

You may prefer your answer in degrees and fractions of degrees rather than degrees, minutes, and seconds. The necessary program changes are listed following the example below.

Example:

How many degrees are there in an angle of 2.5 radians?

```
ANGLE CONVERSION: RADIANS TO DEGREES

(ENTER 0 TO END THIS PROGRAM)
ANGLE IN RADIANS? 2.5

   DEGREES = 143

ANGLE IN RADIANS? 0

1 REM - OPTION 110-120
5 GRAPHICS 0
6 PI=3.1415927
10 PRINT "ANGLE CONVERSION: RADIANS TO DEGREES"
   :
109 REM - CALCULATE DEGREES OF ANGLE WITHIN 360 DEGREES, PRINT
110 PRINT "   DEGREES = ";
120 PRINT INT((D-360*D1)*100+0.5)/100
150 PRINT
   :
170 END
```

Angle Conversion: Degrees to Radians

This program converts an angle given in degrees, minutes, and seconds to radians.

Examples:

An angle measures 30 degrees, 5 minutes, and 3 seconds. What would be the measure of this angle in radians?

What would be the radian measurement of two angles measuring 278 degrees, 19 minutes, 54 seconds and 721 degrees, 0 minutes, 0 seconds?

```
ANGLE CONVERSION: DEGREES TO RADIANS

(TO END, ENTER 0,0,0)
ANGLE IN DEGREES, MINUTES, SECONDS:
? 30,5,3
RADIANS =0.5250676851

ANGLE IN DEGREES, MINUTES, SECONDS:
? 278,19,54
RADIANS =4.85780328

ANGLE IN DEGREES, MINUTES, SECONDS:
? 721,0,0
RADIANS =0.01745149

ANGLE IN DEGREES, MINUTES, SECONDS:
? 0,0,0

5 GRAPHICS 0
10 PRINT "ANGLE CONVERSION: DEGREES TO RADIANS"
20 PRINT
30 PRINT "(TO END, ENTER 0,0,0)"
40 PRINT "ANGLE IN DEGREES, ";
45 PRINT "MINUTES, SECONDS:"
50 INPUT D,M,S
59 REM - TEST FOR END OF PROGRAM
60 IF D<>0 THEN 100
70 IF M<>0 THEN 100
80 IF S<>0 THEN 100
90 GOTO 150
99 REM - CONVERT DEGREES, MINUTES, SECONDS TO DEGREES
100 A=D+M/60+S/3600
109 REM - CALCULATE NUMBER OF COMPLETE CIRCLES
110 R=INT(A/360)
119 REM - CALCULATE ANGLE WITHIN 360 DEGREES, PRINT
120 PRINT "RADIANS =";
125 PRINT A*0.01745329-R*6.2831853
130 PRINT
```

```
30 DIM X(91),Y(90)
31 REM
38 REM - N IS THE NUMBER OF POINTS
39 REM - TO BE CALCULATED
40 N=90
48 REM - ABSOLUTE VALUE OF ALL
49 REM - ENDPOINTS ARE EQUAL
50 PRINT "ABSOLUTE VALUE OF ENDPOINTS";
60 INPUT Z
70 PRINT
75 X1=15
76 Y1=18
77 REM - CALCULATE INCREMENTS OF AXES
78 REM - ACCORDING TO CHARACTERS
79 REM - PER AXIS
80 PRINT "INCREMENT OF X-AXIS =";Z/X1
90 PRINT "INCREMENT OF Y-AXIS =";Z/Y1
100 PRINT
102 PRINT "* * * PLEASE WAIT A FEW MINUTES * * *"
104 PRINT "         FOR THE GRAPH TO APPEAR"
108 REM - E IS THE NEXT PRINT LOCATION
109 E=1
110 FOR I=1 TO N
119 REM - CONVERT DEGREES TO RADIANS
120 D=0.06981317*I
127 REM - ENTER FUNCTION IN LINE 130
128 REM - AS A FUNCTION OF 'D'
129 REM - ("130 F='FUNCTION'")
130 F=2*(1-COS(D))
137 REM - CALCULATE EACH CARTESIAN
138 REM - COORDINATE, ROUND OFF TO
139 REM - NEAREST INCREMENT ON AXIS
140 X(I)=INT(((F*COS(D)/Z+1)*X1)+0.5)
150 Y(I)=INT(((-F*SIN(D)/Z+1)*Y1)+0.5)
160 NEXT I
165 REM
167 REM - SORT COORDINATES; REORDER
168 REM -    Y(1) TO Y(N) SMALLEST
169 REM -         TO LARGEST
170 FOR J=1 TO N
180 FOR I=1 TO N-J
190 A=X(I)
200 B=Y(I)
210 IF B<=Y(I+1) THEN 260
220 X(I)=X(I+1)
230 Y(I)=Y(I+1)
240 X(I+1)=A
250 Y(I+1)=B
260 NEXT I
270 NEXT J
278 REM - NEXT POINT TO BE PLOTTED
279 REM - IS STORED IN 'T'
280 T=1
288 REM - SKIP POINTS OUT OF THE
289 REM - Y-POSITIVE RANGE
```

```
290 FOR P=0 TO N-1
300 IF Y(P+1)>=0 THEN 320
310 NEXT P
318 REM - LOOP TO CALL UP EACH Y-
319 REM - INCREMENT FOR LINES OF PRINT
320 FOR I=0 TO Y1*2
330 T=T+P
337 REM - NUMBER OF POINTS TO BE
338 REM - PLOTTED ON EACH LINE
339 REM - STORED IN P
340 P=0
349 REM - ALL POINTS PLOTTED?
350 IF T>N THEN 370
359 REM - Y-VALUE ON Y-LINE?
360 IF Y(T)=I THEN 420
369 REM - PRINT X-AXIS
370 IF I=Y1 THEN 400
379 REM - PRINT Y-AXIS
380 Z=X1:GOSUB 950
385 PRINT CHR$(124);:REM VERT. BAR
386 E=E+1
390 GOTO 860
400 S=N+1
410 GOTO 740
418 REM - NEXT POINT TO BE PLOTTED
419 REM - ON SAME LINE?
420 FOR L=T TO N
430 IF Y(L)>Y(T) THEN 450
440 P=P+1
450 NEXT L
460 IF P=1 THEN 560
467 REM - LOOP TO SORT X-COORDINATES
468 REM - WITH EQUAL Y-COORDINATES;
469 REM - REORDER SMALLEST TO LARGEST
470 FOR J=1 TO P
480 FOR L=1 TO P-J
490 C=X(T+L-1)
500 A=X(T+L)
510 IF C<=A THEN 540
520 X(T+L-1)=A
530 X(T+L)=C
540 NEXT L
550 NEXT J
559 REM - PRINT X-AXIS?
560 IF I=Y1 THEN 730
570 L=-1
580 S=0
587 REM - MORE THAN ONE POINT TO
588 REM - BE PLOTTED AT SAME POINT
589 REM - ON GRAPH?
590 FOR K=0 TO P-1
600 IF X(T+K)=L THEN 690
610 L=X(T+K)
618 REM - PLOT POINT TO THE LEFT
619 REM - OF Y-AXIS?
```

```
620 IF L=X1 THEN 660
630 IF L<X1 THEN 670
640 IF S=1 THEN 670
649 REM - PRINT Y-AXIS
650 Z=X1:GOSUB 950
655 PRINT CHR$(124);:REM VERT. BAR
656 E=E+1
660 S=1
668 REM - POINT OUTSIDE OF
669 REM - X-POSITIVE RANGE?
670 IF L>X1*2 THEN 860
679 REM - PLOT POINT
680 Z=L:GOSUB 950
685 PRINT "*";
686 E=E+1
690 NEXT K
700 IF S=1 THEN 860
709 REM - PRINT Y-AXIS
710 Z=X1:GOSUB 950
715 PRINT CHR$(124);:REM VERT. BAR
716 E=E+1
720 GOTO 860
730 S=T
739 REM - LOOP TO PRINT LINE OF X-AXIS
740 FOR J=0 TO X1*2
750 IF X(S)<>J THEN 830
759 REM - PLOT POINT ON X-AXIS
760 PRINT "*";
761 F=F+1
770 K=S
780 IF K>T+P-1 THEN 840
790 IF X(K)<>X(S) THEN 820
800 K=K+1
810 GOTO 780
820 S=K
825 GOTO 840
829 REM - PRINT X-AXIS
830 PRINT CHR$(18);:REM HORZ. BAR
831 E=E+1
840 NEXT J
849 REM - LABEL X-AXIS
850 PRINT "X";
860 PRINT
861 REM - NEW LINE, RESET PRINT LOC.
862 E=1
870 NEXT I
879 REM - LABEL Y-AXIS
880 Z=X1:GOSUB 950
885 PRINT "Y"
890 GOTO 999
900 REM - SUBROUTINE TO TAB
910 REM - Z IS TAB LOCATION,
920 REM - E IS CURRENT
950 IF Z-E<1 THEN 990
960 PRINT " ";
```

```
970  E=E+1
980  GOTO 950
990  RETURN
999  END
```

Plot of Functions

This program calculates and plots up to nine functions. All functions must be functions of x, and all will be plotted on the same set of axes.

To set up the axes you must input the endpoints of the x and y axes. You must also state the increment by which the points on each axis are to be increased.

The graph is unconventional in that its x axis runs vertically while its y axis runs horizontally. To read the graph you must either turn your output 90 degrees counterclockwise or mentally adjust to the change in convention.

The graph is also unconventional in that its axes do not necessarily cross at zero. A reminder as to where the axes cross is printed at the top of each graph.

You must enter the functions to be plotted as program statements prior to running the program. Statement numbers 221 to 229 are reserved for this purpose. Functions must be entered in the number sequence $Y(1)$, $Y(2)$,...,$Y(9)$. For example, if you wish to plot the functions $f(x) = 2x + 1$ and $f(x) = \sqrt{x}$, you must type:

```
221  Y(1)=2*X+1
222  Y(2)=SQR(X)
```

The length of the y axis is limited by the width of your output device. This program tests for a length not to exceed the width of the Atari screen. The test at statement 140 should be altered to accommodate your particular output device. For example, an output device with a line width of 64 characters will accommodate a graph 62 spaces wide. You would change statement 140 to:

```
140  IF Y2<=62 THEN 170
```

Example:

Plot the equations $f(x) = \cos(x)$ and $f(x) = \sin(x)$.

PLOT OF FUNCTIONS

NUMBER OF FUNCTIONS? 2
X-AXIS: LOWER ENDPOINT,
UPPER ENDPOINT,INCREMENT? -5,5,0.25
Y-AXIS: LEFT ENDPOINT,
RIGHT ENDPOINT, INCREMENT? -2,2,0.1

X-AXIS CROSSES Y-AXIS AT Y=-2
Y AXIS CROSSES X-AXIS AT X=-5

```
+++++++++++++++++++++++++1++++++2++++++++++Y
+                        1              2
+                      1                2
+                    1                 2
+                   1                 2
+                  1                 2
+                 1                 2
+               1               2
+               1             2
+              1           2
+             1 2
+             2 1
+            2     1
+           2       1
+           2         1
+          2             1
+         2             1
+        2                1
+         2                1
+           2                1
+             2               1
+               2             1
+                2            1
+                   2      1
+                       *
+                   1   2
+                 1     2
+               1         2
+             1          2
+           1           2
+          1           2
+         1       2
+        1      2
+        1         2
+        1    2
+        1  2
+          1 2
+           21
+        2     1
+       2        1
+       2          1
+       2              1
X
```

```
5 GRAPHICS O
10 PRINT "PLOT OF FUNCTIONS"
20 PRINT
29 REM - NUMBER OF FUNCTIONS WHICH CAN BE PLOTTED IS LIMITED TO 9
30 DIM Y(9),A$(11)
40 A$="123456789++"
69 REM - STATEMENTS 79 TO 120 REQUEST USER INPUT
70 PRINT "NUMBER OF FUNCTIONS";
80 INPUT N
90 PRINT "X-AXIS: LOWER ENDPOINT,"
95 PRINT "UPPER ENDPOINT,INCREMENT";
100 INPUT X1,X2,X3
110 PRINT "Y-AXIS: LEFT ENDPOINT,"
115 PRINT "RIGHT ENDPOINT, INCREMENT";
120 INPUT Y1,Y2,Y3
129 REM - CALCULATE NUMBER OF SPACES ON Y-AXIS
130 Y2=(Y2-Y1)/Y3
138 REM - TEST FOR A Y-AXIS TOO LONG FOR OUTPUT DEVICE
139 REM - IF YES; THEN LESSEN RANGE OR INCREASE INCREMENT
140 IF Y2<=36 THEN 170
150 PRINT "Y-RANGE TOO LARGE"
160 GOTO 110
170 PRINT
180 PRINT
189 REM - MAKE NOTE OF WHERE AXES CROSS
190 PRINT "X-AXIS CROSSES Y-AXIS ";
195 PRINT "AT Y=";Y1
200 PRINT "Y AXIS CROSSES X-AXIS ";
210 PRINT "AT X=";X1:PRINT
219 REM - SET UP LOOP TO READ VALUE AT EACH X-INCREMENT
220 FOR X=X1 TO X2 STEP X3
221 REM - FUNCTIONS Y(1) TO Y(9) SHOULD BE ENTERED AT LINES 221 TO 229
230 FOR I=1 TO N
239 REM - ESTABLISH THE ROUNDED VALUE OF Y FOR EACH X-INCREMENT VALUE
240 Y(I)=INT((Y(I)-Y1)/Y3+0.5)
250 NEXT I
259 REM - LOOP TO READ VALUE OF EACH Y-INCREMENT
260 FOR I=0 TO Y2
269 REM - S COUNTS THE NUMBER OF VALUES AT EACH Y-INCREMENT FOR EACH X
270 S=0
280 FOR J=1 TO N
289 REM - PLOT A POINT ON THIS SPOT? IF YES, STORE FUNCTION NUMBER IN T
290 IF Y(J)<>I THEN 320
300 S=S+1
310 T=J
320 NEXT J
327 REM - TEST FOR NUMBER OF POINTS TO PLOT ON EACH SPOT;
328 REM - IF O PRINT "+" (FIRST LINE ONLY), IF 1 PRINT FUNCTION NUMBER,
329 REM - IF 2 OR MORE PRINT "*"
330 IF S>0 THEN 360
340 PRINT A$(SGN(I)+10,SGN(I)+10);
350 GOTO 400
360 IF S>1 THEN 390
370 PRINT A$(T,T);
380 GOTO 400
```

```
390 PRINT "*";
400 NEXT I
409 REM - LABEL AXES AT THE LAST SPACE ON EACH AXIS
410 IF X>X1 THEN 430
420 PRINT "Y";
429 REM - ADVANCE PRINTER TO NEXT LINE
430 PRINT
439 REM - PRINT SPACE INSTEAD OF "+" AFTER FIRST LINE OF PRINT (Y-AXIS)
440 A$(11)=" "
450 NEXT X
460 PRINT "X"
470 END
```

Linear Interpolation

This program calculates the *y* coordinates of points on a line given their *x* coordinates. It is necessary to know coordinates of two points on the same line.

The point is interpolated using the following formula:

$$y = y_1 + \frac{(y_2 - y_1) \cdot (x - x_1)}{(x_2 - x_1)}$$

where: x_1, y_1 = coordinates of first point on the line
x_2, y_2 = coordinates of second point on the line
x = abscissa of point to be interpolated
y = ordinate of the point on the line with x

Examples:

A conversion table lists 60°F as 15.56°C and 90°F as 32.22°C. Calculate degrees Celsius of 73°F and 85.6°F.

A new sales tax of 17.5% has been imposed on us. What will be the tax on a sofa which sells for $455.68?

```
LINEAR INTERPOLATION

X,Y OF FIRST POINT? 60,15.56
X,Y OF SECOND POINT? 90,32.22
INTERPOLATE:X = ? 73
          Y =   22.779

MORE POINTS (1=YES, 0=NO)? 1

INTERPOLATE:X = ? 85.6
          Y =   29.777

MORE POINTS (1=YES, 0=NO)? 0

NEW LINE (1=YES, 0=NO)? 1

X,Y OF FIRST POINT? 0,0
X,Y OF SECOND POINT? 100,17.5
INTERPOLATE:X = ? 455.68
          Y =   79.744

MORE POINTS (1=YES, 0=NO)? 0

NEW LINE (1=YES, 0=NO)? 0

5 GRAPHICS 0
10 PRINT "LINEAR INTERPOLATION"
20 PRINT
29 REM - ENTER X- AND Y-COORDINATES OF TWO POINTS ON THE LINE
30 PRINT "X,Y OF FIRST POINT";
```

```
40  INPUT X1,Y1
50  PRINT "X,Y OF SECOND POINT";
60  INPUT X2,Y2
69  REM - ENTER X-COORDINATE OF POINT TO BE INTERPOLATED
70  PRINT "INTERPOLATE:X = ";
80  INPUT X
89  REM - COMPUTE CORRESPONDING Y-COORDINATE
90  Y=Y1+(Y2-Y1)/(X2-X1)*(X-X1)
99  REM - ROUND OFF, PRINT
100 PRINT "              Y =   ";
101 PRINT INT(Y*1000+0.5)/1000
110 PRINT
120 PRINT "MORE POINTS (1=YES, 0=NO)";
130 INPUT Z
140 PRINT
150 IF Z=1 THEN 70
159 REM - INTERPOLATE ON ANOTHER LINE?
160 PRINT "NEW LINE (1=YES, 0=NO)";
170 INPUT Z
180 IF Z=1 THEN 20
190 END
```

Curvilinear Interpolation

This program computes y coordinates of points on a curve given their x coordinates. You must input coordinates of known points on the curve, no two having the same abscissa.

The computations are performed using the Lagrange method of interpolation.

The number of known points on the curve which may be entered in the program is limited to 50. You may increase or decrease this limit by altering statement 30 according to the following scheme:

```
30 DIM X( P ),Y( P )
```

where P = the number of known points on a curve.

Examples:

Consider the curve $y = x^3 - 3x + 3$. You know that the points $(-3,-15)$, $(-2,1)$, $(-1,5)$, $(0,3)$, $(1,1)$, $(2,5)$, and $(3,21)$ are on the curve. What is the value of y when $x = -1.65$ and 0.2?

Given the following points from a sine curve, what is the sine of -2.47 and the sine of 1.5?

$(-5,0.958)$	$(0,0)$
$(-4,0.757)$	$(1,0.841)$
$(-3,-0.141)$	$(2,0.909)$
$(-2,-0.909)$	$(3,0.141)$
$(-1,-0.841)$	$(4,-0.757)$
	$(5,-0.959)$

```
CURVILINEAR INTERPOLATION

NUMBER OF KNOWN POINTS? 7
X,Y OF POINT 1? -3,-15
X,Y OF POINT 2? -2,1
X,Y OF POINT 3? -1,5
X,Y OF POINT 4? 0,3
X,Y OF POINT 5? 1,1
X,Y OF POINT 6? 2,5
X,Y OF POINT 7? 3,21

INTERPOLATE: X= ? -1.65
             Y=   3.45787496

MORE POINTS HERE (1=YES, 0=NO)? 1

INTERPOLATE: X= ? 0.2
             Y=   2.40799992

MORE POINTS HERE (1=YES, 0=NO)? 0
ANOTHER CURVE (1=YES, 0=NO)? 1
NUMBER OF KNOWN POINTS? 11
X,Y OF POINT 1? -5,0.958
X,Y OF POINT 2? -4,0.757
X,Y OF POINT 3? -3,-0.141
X,Y OF POINT 4? -2,-0.909
```

```
X,Y OF POINT 5? -1,-0.841
X,Y OF POINT 6? 0,0
X,Y OF POINT 7? 1,0.841
X,Y OF POINT 8? 2,0.909
X,Y OF POINT 9? 3,0.141
X,Y OF POINT 10? 4,-0.757
X,Y OF POINT 11? 5,-0.959


INTERPOLATE: X= ? -2.47
             Y=  -0.6218395827


MORE POINTS HERE (1=YES, 0=NO)? 1

INTERPOLATE: X= ? 1.5
             Y=   0.9971637861


MORE POINTS HERE (1=YES, 0=NO)? 0
ANOTHER CURVE (1=YES, 0=NO)? 0

5 GRAPHICS 0
10 PRINT "CURVILINEAR INTERPOLATION"
20 PRINT
28 REM - LIMIT X() AND Y() TO MAXIMUM NUMBER OF POINTS KNOWN ON ANY
29 REM - CURVE TO BE ENTERED
30 DIM X(50),Y(50)
40 PRINT "NUMBER OF KNOWN POINTS";
50 INPUT P
60 FOR I=1 TO P
69 REM - ENTER COORDINATES OF KNOWN POINTS ON CURVE
70 PRINT "X,Y OF POINT ";I;
80 INPUT X1,Y1
82 X(I)=X1
84 Y(I)=Y1
90 NEXT I
100 PRINT
109 REM - ENTER X-COORDINATE OF POINT TO BE INTERPOLATED
110 PRINT "INTERPOLATE: X= ";
120 INPUT A
130 B=0
138 REM - COMPUTE CORRESPONDING Y-COORDINATES BY LAGRANGE METHOD OF
139 REM - INTERPOLATION
140 FOR J=1 TO P
150 T=1
160 FOR I=1 TO P
170 IF I=J THEN 190
180 T=T*(A-X(I))/(X(J)-X(I))
190 NEXT I
200 B=B+T*Y(J)
210 NEXT J
219 REM - PRINT RESULTS
220 PRINT "                    Y=   ";B
230 PRINT
239 REM - INTERPOLATE MORE POINTS ON SAME CURVE?
240 PRINT "MORE POINTS HERE ";
245 PRINT "(1=YES, 0=NO)";
```

```
250  INPUT C
260  IF C=1 THEN 100
269  REM - RESTART OR END PROGRAM?
270  PRINT "ANOTHER CURVE ";
275  PRINT "(1=YES, 0=NO)";
280  INPUT C
290  IF C=1 THEN 40
300  END
```

Integration: Simpson's Rule

This program approximates the definite integral of a function. The integral is computed using Simpson's rule.

The method the program takes is optional: you must supply either the function of the curve or values of the function at specified intervals. For both methods you must enter the limits of integration and the increment between points within the limits.

If the function to be integrated is known, it must be entered before running the program. The function will be defined at line 350. For example, the function $f(x) = x^3$ will be entered as follows:

```
350 F=X^3
```

Examples:

Find the definite integral of the function $f(x) = x^3$ between 0 and 2 with increments of 0.2 and 0.1.

What is the integral of a curve between -1 and 1 if the points known are as follows:

$(-1, 0.54)$	$(0.25, 0.969)$
$(-0.75, 0.73)$	$(0.5, 0.878)$
$(-0.5, 0.878)$	$(0.75, .073)$
$(-0.25, 0.969)$	$(1, 0.54)$
$(0, 1)$	

```
INTEGRATION: SIMPSON'S RULE

FORMULA:(1=KNOWN, 0=UNKNOWN)? 1
THE LOWER, UPPER LIMITS? 0,2
INCREMENT OF X? 0.2
INTEGRAL IS 3.99999994


5 GRAPHICS 0
10 PRINT "INTEGRATION: SIMPSON'S RULE"
20 PRINT
30 PRINT "FORMULA:(1=KNOWN, 0=UNKNOWN)";
40 INPUT S
60 PRINT "THE LOWER, UPPER LIMITS";
70 INPUT A,B
80 PRINT "INCREMENT OF X";
90 INPUT X1
98 REM - INCREMENT MUST DIVIDE INTERVAL INTO EQUAL SUBINTERVALS;
99 REM - IF NOT, CHANGE INCREMENT
100 IF (B-A)/X1<>INT((B-A)/X1) THEN 800
110 IF S=1 THEN 150
119 REM - FORMULA NOT KNOWN; ENTER FUNCTION VALUE AT INTEGRATION LIMITS
120 PRINT "FIRST, LAST VALUE OF F(X)";
130 INPUT Y1,Y2
140 GOTO 170
149 REM - FORMULA KNOWN; CALCULATE F(X) AT INTEGRATION LIMITS
150 X=A
152 GOSUB 350
154 Y1=F
```

```
160  X=B
162  GOSUB 350
164  Y2=F
170  C=0
180  D=0
189  REM - LOOP FOR EACH INTERVAL
190  FOR I=1 TO (B-A)/X1-0.5
200  IF S=1 THEN 240
209  REM - ENTER KNOWN FUNCTION VALUE AT EACH INTERVAL
210  PRINT "VALUE OF F(X) AT: "
211  PRINT "              INTERVAL ";I;
212  PRINT "  (X=";A+I*X1;")";
220  INPUT Y
230  GOTO 250
239  REM - CALCULATE F(X) AT EACH SUBINTERVAL
240  X=A+I*X1
242  GOSUB 350
244  Y=F
249  REM - INTERVAL EVEN OR ODD?
250  T2=I/2:R=INT(T2)
255  IF T2=R THEN 280
259  REM - SUM ALL ODD-INTERVAL FUNCTION VALUES
260  C=C+Y
270  GOTO 290
279  REM - SUM ALL EVEN-INTERVAL FUNCTION VALUES
280  D=D+Y
290  NEXT I
299  REM - COMPUTE INTEGRAL; PRINT
300  PRINT "INTEGRAL IS ";
310  PRINT X1/3*(Y1+(C*4)+D*2+Y2)
320  GOTO 999
330  REM - DEFINE KNOWN FUNCTION
340  REM - BELOW: "F='FUNCTION(X)'"
350  F=X^3
360  RETURN
999  END
```

Integration: Trapezoidal Rule

This program approximates the definite integral of a function. The integral is computed using the trapezoidal rule. You must provide the limits of integration and the number of intervals within the limits.

The function to be integrated must be entered before running the program. The function of x will be defined at line 210. For example, the function $f(x) = x^3$ will be entered as follows:

```
210 F=X^3
```

Examples:

Find the definite integral of the function $f(x) = x^3$ between 0 and 2 with 10 and 20 intervals.

Find the definite integral of the function $f(x) = x^{-2}$ between 1 and 2 and 2 and 3 using 10 subintervals.

```
INTEGRATION: TRAPEZOIDAL RULE

(ENTER 0,0 TO END PROGRAM)
LOWER, UPPER LIMITS? 0,2
NUMBER OF INTERVALS? 10
INTEGRAL = 4.03999994

LOWER, UPPER LIMITS? 0,2
NUMBER OF INTERVALS? 20
INTEGRAL = 4.00999994

LOWER, UPPER LIMITS? 0,0

5 GRAPHICS 0
10 PRINT "INTEGRATION: TRAPEZOIDAL RULE"
20 PRINT
40 PRINT "(ENTER 0,0 TO END PROGRAM)"
50 PRINT "LOWER, UPPER LIMITS";
60 INPUT A,B
69 REM - END PROGRAM?
70 IF A=B THEN 230
80 PRINT "NUMBER OF INTERVALS";
90 INPUT N
100 I=0
109 REM - D IS THE SIZE OF EACH INTERVAL
110 D=(B-A)/N
119 REM - ADD UP THE AREA OF EACH TRAPEZOID
120 FOR X=A TO B STEP D
122 GOSUB 210
130 I=I+F
140 NEXT X
141 REM - OBTAIN FUNCTION OF A
142 X=A
143 GOSUB 210
```

```
144 A=F
145 REM - OBTAIN FUNCTION OF B
146 X=B
147 GOSUB 210
148 B=F
149 REM - COMPUTE INTEGRAL, PRINT
150 I=(I-(A+B)/2)*D
160 PRINT "INTEGRAL = ";I
170 PRINT
179 REM - RESTART PROGRAM
180 GOTO 50
190 REM - ENTER FUNCTION BELOW:
200 REM - "F=´FUNCTION(X)´"
210 F=X^3
220 RETURN
230 END
```

Integration: Gaussian Quadrature

This program approximates the definite integral of a function. You must provide the limits of integration and the number of intervals within the limits.

The interval of integration is divided into equal subintervals. The definite integral is computed over each subinterval using Gauss' formula. The integrals of the subintervals are summed to give the definite integral of the full interval.

You must enter the function to be integrated before running the program. The function of x will be defined at line 350. For example, the function $f(x) = x^3$ will be entered as follows:

```
350 F=Z^3
```

Examples:

Find the definite integral of the function $f(x) = x^3$ between 0 and 2 with 10 and 20 subintervals.

Find the definite integral of the function $f(x) = x^{-2}$ between 1 and 2 and 2 and 3 using 10 subintervals.

```
INTEGRATION: GAUSSIAN QUADRATURE

LOWER, UPPER LIMITS? 0,2
NUMBER OF INTERVALS? 10
INTEGRAL =3.99999993

CHANGE DATA AND RECOMPUTE?
(0=NO,1=LIMITS,2=INTERVALS)? 2
NUMBER OF INTERVALS? 20
INTEGRAL =3.99999993

CHANGE DATA AND RECOMPUTE?
(0=NO,1=LIMITS,2=INTERVALS)? 0

5 GRAPHICS 0
10 PRINT "INTEGRATION: GAUSSIAN QUADRATURE"
20 PRINT
30 REM - ENTER FUNCTION IN LINE 350
39 REM - ABSCISSAS AND WEIGHT FACTORS FOR 20-POINT GUASSIAN INTEGRATION
40 DATA .076526521,.15275339,.22778585
45 DATA .14917299,.37370609,.14209611
50 DATA .510867,.13168864,.63605368
55 DATA .11819453,.74633191,.10193012
60 DATA .83911697,.083276742,.91223443
65 DATA .062672048,.96397193,.04060143
70 DATA .9931286,.017614007
80 PRINT "LOWER, UPPER LIMITS";
90 INPUT X,Y
100 PRINT "NUMBER OF INTERVALS";
110 INPUT N
120 S=(Y-X)/N/2
130 T=X+S
```

```
140 R=0
149 REM - COMPUTE INTEGRAL FOR EACH SUBINTERVAL
150 FOR I=1 TO N
160 P=0
169 REM - COMPUTE SUMMATION FACTOR FOR EACH SUBINTERVAL
170 FOR J=1 TO 10
180 READ A,B
190 Z=S*A+T
192 GOSUB 350
194 Z1=F
196 Z=T-S*A
197 GOSUB 350
198 P=P+B*(Z1+F)
200 NEXT J
210 RESTORE
220 R=R+P*S
230 T=T+2*S
240 NEXT I
250 PRINT "INTEGRAL =";R
260 PRINT
270 PRINT "CHANGE DATA AND RECOMPUTE?"
280 PRINT "(0=NO,1=LIMITS,2=INTERVALS)";
290 INPUT S
300 IF S=1 THEN 80
310 IF S=2 THEN 100
320 GOTO 370
330 REM - ENTER FUNCTION BELOW:
340 REM - "F='FUNCTION(Z)'"
350 F=Z^3
360 RETURN
370 END
```

Derivative

This program calculates the derivative of a given function at a given point.

You must enter the function being evaluated before you run the program. The function will be entered in a statement at line 180. For example, to evaluate the equation $f(x) = x^{-2} + \cos(x)$ you would enter the following:

```
180 F=Z^2+COS(Z)
```

Example:

Calculate the derivative of the equation $x^2 + \cos(x) = 0$ when $x = -1$, $x = 0$, and $x = 1$.

```
DERIVATIVE

(ENTER X=99999 TO END)
DERIVATIVE AT X=? -1
                IS -1.15856168
DERIVATIVE AT X=? 0
                IS -1.0239954E-05
DERIVATIVE AT X=? 1
                IS 1.15852584
DERIVATIVE AT X=? 99999

5 GRAPHICS O
10 PRINT "DERIVATIVE"
20 PRINT
40 PRINT "(ENTER X=99999 TO END)"
50 PRINT "DERIVATIVE AT X=";
60 INPUT X1
69 REM - TEST FOR END OF PROGRAM
70 IF X1=99999 THEN 200
80 D=0
89 REM - CALCULATE DIFFERENCE QUOTIENTS FOR POINTS APPROACHING X
90 FOR N=1 TO 10
100 D1=D
110 X=X1+0.5^N
111 REM - OBTAIN FUNCTION OF X
112 Z=X
113 GOSUB 180
114 REM - STORE RESULT IN Z1
115 Z1=F
116 REM - OBTAIN FUNCTION OF X1
117 Z=X1
118 GOSUB 180
119 Y=Z1-F
120 D=Y/(X-X1)
130 NEXT N
138 REM - APPROXIMATE DERIVATIVE
```

```
139 REM - OF FUNCTION AT X, PRINT
140 PRINT "                    IS ";2*D-D1
149 REM - RESTART PROGRAM
150 GOTO 50
160 REM - ENTER FUNCTION BELOW:
170 REM - "F='FUNCTION(Z)'"
180 F=Z^2+COS(Z)
190 RETURN
200 END
```

Roots of Quadratic Equations

This program calculates the roots of a quadratic equation. The equation must be in the following form:

$$ax^2 + bx + c = 0$$

where a, b, c are real coefficients.

The formula used to calculate the roots is:

$$\text{root} = \frac{-b \pm \sqrt{b^2 - 4 \cdot a \cdot c}}{2 \cdot a}$$

Example:

Compute the roots of the following equations:

$$2x^2 + x - 1 = 0$$
$$x^2 + 4x + 6 = 0$$

```
ROOTS OF QUADRATIC EQUATIONS

COEFFICIENTS A,B,C? 2,1,-1
ROOTS (REAL):
-1,0.5

MORE DATA (1=YES, 0=NO)? 1

COEFFICIENTS A,B,C? 1,4,6
ROOTS (COMPLEX):
-2 +OR- 1.41421359 I

MORE DATA (1=YES, 0=NO)? 0
```

```
5 GRAPHICS 0
10 PRINT "ROOTS OF QUADRATIC EQUATIONS"
20 PRINT
30 PRINT "COEFFICIENTS A,B,C";
40 INPUT A,B,C
50 S=B^2-4*A*C
60 R=SQR(ABS(S))
70 IF S<0 THEN 100
80 PRINT "ROOTS (REAL): "
82 PRINT (-B-R)/(2*A);
85 PRINT ",";(-B+R)/(2*A)
90 GOTO 110
100 PRINT "ROOTS (COMPLEX): "
102 PRINT -B/(2*A);
105 PRINT " +OR- ";R/(2*A);" I"
110 PRINT
120 PRINT "MORE DATA (1=YES, 0=NO)";
130 INPUT X
140 IF X=1 THEN 20
150 END
```

Real Roots of Polynomials: Newton

This program calculates real roots of a polynomial with real coefficients. You must give an estimate of each root.

The calculations are performed using Newton's method for approximating roots of equations. The value of the error and derivative are included for each root calculated.

The equation you enter is presently limited to a degree of 10. You may enter a larger degree of equation by altering statements 30 and 40 of the program according to the following scheme:

```
30 DIM A(N+1),B(N+1)
40 FOR I=1 TO N+1
```

where N = degree of equation.

Example:

Find the roots of $4x^4 - 2.5x^2 - x + 0.5$.

```
REAL ROOTS OF POLYNOMIALS: NEWTON
DEGREE OF EQUATION? 4

COEFFICIENT A(0)? 0.5
COEFFICIENT A(1)? -1
COEFFICIENT A(2)? -2.5
COEFFICIENT A(3)? 0
COEFFICIENT A(4)? 4
GUESS? -0.8
ROOT        = 0.3035763403
ERROR       = -1E-10
DERIVATIVE = -2.07024701


NEW VALUE (1=YES, 0=NO)? 0
NEW FUNCTION (1=YES, 0=NO)? 0

5 GRAPHICS 0
10 PRINT "REAL ROOTS OF POLYNOMIALS: NEWTON"
11 REM - LIMIT A() AND B() TO N+1;
12 REM - WHEN THIS IS DONE, LOOP AT
13 REM - LINE 40 SHOULD BE SET TO
14 REM - COUNT FROM 1 TO N+1
15 DIM A(11),B(11)
20 PRINT
39 REM - INITIALIZE ARRAY VARIABLES
40 FOR I=1 TO 11
50 A(I)=0
60 B(I)=0
70 NEXT I
80 PRINT "DEGREE OF EQUATION";
90 INPUT N
95 PRINT
```

```
100 FOR I=1 TO N+1
108 REM - ENTER COEFFICIENTS IN ORDER
109 REM - OF LESSER TO HIGHER DEGREE
110 PRINT "COEFFICIENT A(";I-1;")";
120 INPUT A1
122 A(I)=A1
130 NEXT I
140 FOR I=1 TO 10
148 REM - CALCULATE COEFFICIENT OF
149 REM - DERIVATIVE OF POLYNOMIAL
150 B(I)=A(I+1)*I
160 NEXT I
170 PRINT
179 REM - INITIALIZE GUESS
180 PRINT "GUESS";
190 INPUT X
200 Q=0
210 S=1
220 F1=0
230 F0=0
239 REM - COUNT ITERATIONS
240 Q=Q+1
250 FOR I=1 TO N+1
259 REM - CALCULATE VALUE OF FUNCTION
260 F0=F0+A(I)*S
269 REM - CALC. VALUE OF DERIVATIVE
270 F1=F1+B(I)*S
280 S=S*X
290 NEXT I
298 REM - TEST FOR A ZERO DERIVATIVE;
299 REM - IF YES, STOP SEARCH, PRINT
300 IF F1=0 THEN 360
308 REM - GET NEW GUESS USING
309 REM - PREVIOUS GUESS
310 S=X-F0/F1
318 REM - IF NEW GUESS EQUALS LAST
319 REM - GUESS, STOP SEARCH, PRINT
320 IF X=S THEN 380
329 REM - SAVE LAST GUESS
330 X=S
340 IF Q>100 THEN 490
350 GOTO 210
360 PRINT "DERIVATIVE = 0 AT X = ";X
370 GOTO 180
380 PRINT
390 PRINT "ROOT       = ";X
395 PRINT "ERROR      = ";F0
400 PRINT "DERIVATIVE = ";F1
410 PRINT
418 REM - RERUN TO FIND ANOTHER ROOT
419 REM - IN SAME FUNCTION?
420 PRINT "NEW VALUE (1=YES, 0=NO)";
430 INPUT A
440 IF A=1 THEN 170
449 REM - RESTART OR END PROGRAM?
```

```
450 PRINT "NEW FUNCTION (1=YES, 0=NO)";
460 INPUT A
470 IF A=1 THEN 40
480 GOTO 550
487 REM - PRINT CALCULATED VALUES
488 REM - AFTER 100 ITERATIONS;
489 REM - SEARCH 100 MORE?
490 PRINT "100 ITERATIONS COMPLETED:"
500 PRINT "X    = ";X
504 PRINT "F(X) = ";FO
506 PRINT
510 PRINT "CONTINUE (1=YES, 0=NO)";
520 INPUT A
530 IF A=1 THEN 200
540 GOTO 420
550 END
```

Roots of Polynomials: Half-Interval Search

This program calculates roots of polynomials within a given interval. The program first conducts a random search within the given interval for two points with opposite signs. If a change of sign is found, the root is calculated by the half-interval search method. If there is no change of sign found, another interval will be asked for.

Errors may result in this program for two reasons. First, a root may be calculated when it should not be. This may happen if the lowest point is so close to zero that a root is found due to a round-off error. Second, two roots may be so close together that the program never finds the opposite signs between them. The result in this case is that neither root is calculated.

It is necessary to enter the equation before you run the program. The equation will be defined as a function of x at statement 450. For example, if you want to find roots of the function $f(x) = 4x^4 - 2.5x^2 + 0.5$, you will enter:

```
450 F=4*Z^4-2.5*Z^2-Z+0.5
```

Example:

Find a root of the function $f(x) = 4x^4 - 2.5x^2 + 0.5$.

```
ROOTS OF POLYNOMIALS:
HALF-INTERVAL SEARCH

(TO END SEARCH ENTER 0,0)

INTERVAL (LOWER,UPPER)? -1,0
NO CHANGE OF SIGN FOUND
INTERVAL (LOWER,UPPER)? 0,1
ROOT = 0.3035782241

INTERVAL (LOWER,UPPER)? 0,0
```

```
5 GRAPHICS 0
10 PRINT "ROOTS OF POLYNOMIALS: "
15 PRINT "HALF-INTERVAL SEARCH"
20 PRINT
40 DIM D(3)
50 PRINT "(TO END SEARCH ENTER 0,0)"
55 PRINT
59 REM - ESTABLISH INTERVAL OF RANDOM SEARCH
60 PRINT "INTERVAL (LOWER,UPPER)";
70 INPUT A,B
79 REM - TEST FOR USABLE LIMITS ENTERED
80 IF A<>B THEN 120
89 REM - END PROGRAM?
90 IF A=0 THEN 470
100 PRINT "--INTERVAL LIMITS CANNOT BE EQUAL--";
110 GOTO 60
120 IF A<B THEN 150
130 PRINT "--LOWER LIMIT MUST BE ENTERED FIRST--"
```

```
140 GOTO 60
150 Z=A
152 GOSUB 450
154 A1=SGN(F)
160 Z=B
162 GOSUB 450
164 B1=SGN(F)
168 REM - TEST FOR ROOT AT EITHER
169 REM - LIMIT
170 IF A1*B1=0 THEN 360
178 REM - TEST FOR OPPOSITE SIGNS
179 REM - AT INTERVAL LIMITS
180 IF A1*B1<0 THEN 280
188 REM - SEARCH 1000 NUMBERS FOR
189 REM - OPPOSITE SIGNS IN FUNCTION
190 FOR I=1 TO 1000
200 X=A+RND(2)*(B-A)
202 Z=X
204 GOSUB 450
210 X1=SGN(F)
218 REM - TEST FOR ROOT AT RANDOM
219 REM - IF YES, END SEARCH, PRINT
220 IF X1=0 THEN 400
228 REM - TEST FOR OPPOSITE SIGNS AT
229 REM - RANDOM NUMBER & LOWER LIMIT
230 IF A1*X1<0 THEN 270
239 REM - TRY ANOTHER RANDOM NUMBER
240 NEXT I
250 PRINT "NO CHANGE OF SIGN FOUND"
260 GOTO 60
268 REM - CHANGE OF SIGN FOUND;
269 REM - CALCULATE ROOT
270 B=X
277 REM - STORE POSITIVE POINT
278 REM - IN D(1). D(1) AND D(3)
279 REM - BECOME INTERVAL LIMITS
280 D(2+A1)=A
290 D(2-A1)=B
298 REM - CALCULATE MIDPOINT BETWEEN
299 REM - THE TWO LIMITS
300 Y=(D(1)+D(3))/2
302 Z=Y
304 GOSUB 450
310 Y1=SGN(F)
319 REM - TEST FOR ROOT AT MIDPOINT
320 IF Y1=0 THEN 400
328 REM - GET A NEW LIMIT TO CLOSE
329 REM - IN ON ROOT
330 D(2+Y1)=Y
337 REM - TEST FOR A VALUE CLOSE
338 REM - ENOUGH TO ZERO TO ASSUME
339 REM - A ROOT.
340 IF ABS(D(1)-D(3))/ABS(D(1)+ABS(D(3)))<5E-06 THEN 400
349 REM - RETEST WITH NEW LIMITS
350 GOTO 300
```

```
358 REM - ROOT AT AN INTERVAL LIMIT;
359 REM - FIND WHICH LIMIT, PRINT
360 IF A1=0 THEN 390
370 Y=B
380 GOTO 400
390 Y=A
400 PRINT "ROOT = ";Y
410 PRINT
419 REM - RESTART PROGRAM
420 GOTO 60
430 REM - ENTER FUNCTION BELOW:
440 REM - "F=´FUNCTION(Z)´"
450 F=4*Z^4-2.5*Z^2-Z+0.5
460 RETURN
470 END
```

Trig Polynomial

This program solves a trigonometric function for a given angle. The function must be in the following form:

$$f(x) = A_1 \sin(x) + B_1 \cos(x) + A_2 \sin(2x) + B_2 \sin(2x) \ldots + A_n \sin(n \cdot x) + B_n \cos(n \cdot x)$$

where n = the number of pairs of coefficients.

The coefficients of the function are to be entered in a data statement at line 30. The data statement will include the number of pairs of coefficients (n) and the coefficients of the polynomial. It will be entered as follows:

$$\text{30 DATA } n, A_1, B_1, A_2, B_2, \ldots, A_n, B_n$$

Example:

Solve the following equation when the angle equals 45°, 90°, and 105°:

$$f(x) = \sin(x) + 2 \cdot \cos(x) - 2 \cdot \sin(2x) + \cos(2x) + 5 \cdot \sin(3x) - 3 \cdot \cos(3x)$$

```
TRIG POLYNOMIAL
(ENTER ANGLE=99999 TO END)

ANGLE? 45
F(45)=3.09559088

ANGLE? 90
F(90)=-2.83213038

ANGLE? 105
F(105)=-1.54720278

ANGLE? 99999

5 GRAPHICS 0
10 PRINT "TRIG POLYNOMIAL"
20 PRINT
27 REM - ENTER NUMBER OF PAIRS
28 REM - OF TERMS AND COEFFICIENTS
29 REM - WITH DATA STATEMENT
30 PRINT "ENTER NUMBER OF PAIRS OF TERMS AND COEFFICIENTS AT LINE 30!"
40 PRINT "(ENTER ANGLE=99999 TO END)"
45 PRINT
50 PRINT "ANGLE";
60 INPUT R
69 REM - END PROGRAM?
70 IF R=99999 THEN 180
78 REM - GET NUMBER OF PAIRS OF
79 REM - TERMS IN POLYNOMIAL
80 READ N
85 Z=0
```

```
89 REM - READ VALUES OF COEFFICIENTS
90 FOR I=1 TO N
100 READ A,B
108 REM - CALCULATE VALUE OF
109 REM - FUNCTION AT ANGLE X
110 Z=Z+A*SIN(I*R)+B*COS(I*R)
120 NEXT I
129 REM - PRINT RESULTS
130 PRINT "F(";R;")=";Z
138 REM - PREPARE TO REREAD
139 REM - FUNCTION COEFFICIENTS
140 RESTORE
150 PRINT
169 REM - RESTART PROGRAM
170 GOTO 50
180 END
```

Simultaneous Equations

This program solves a system of linear equations. The number of unknown coefficients in each equation must equal the number of equations being solved. You must enter the coefficients of each equation.

The dimension statement at line 30 limits the number of equations which may be solved. You may change this limit according to the following scheme:

$$30 \text{ DIM } A(R, R+1)$$

where R = the maximum number of equations.

Example:

Solve the following system of equations:

$$x + 2x + 3x = 4$$
$$3x + 6x \qquad = 1$$
$$-3x + 4x - 2x = 0$$

```
SIMULTANEOUS EQUATIONS

NUMBER OF EQUATIONS? 3
COEFFICIENT MATRIX:

EQUATION 1
     COEFFICIENT 1? 1
     COEFFICIENT 2? 2
     COEFFICIENT 3? 3
CONSTANT? 4

EQUATION 2
     COEFFICIENT 1? 3
     COEFFICIENT 2? 6
     COEFFICIENT 3? 0
CONSTANT? 1

EQUATION 3
     COEFFICIENT 1? -3
     COEFFICIENT 2? 4
     COEFFICIENT 3? -2
CONSTANT? 0

X1 = -0.356
X2 = 0.344
X3 = 1.222

5 GRAPHICS 0
10 PRINT "SIMULTANEOUS EQUATIONS"
20 PRINT
30 DIM A(15,15)
40 PRINT "NUMBER OF EQUATIONS";
```

```
50  INPUT R
60  PRINT "COEFFICIENT MATRIX:"
70  FOR J=1 TO R
80  PRINT
85  PRINT "EQUATION ";J
90  FOR I=1 TO R+1
100 IF I=R+1 THEN 130
110 PRINT "    COEFFICIENT ";I;
120 GOTO 140
130 PRINT "CONSTANT";
140 INPUT A1
142 A(J,I)=A1
150 NEXT I
160 NEXT J
170 FOR J=1 TO R
180 FOR I=J TO R
190 IF A(I,J)<>0 THEN 230
200 NEXT I
210 PRINT "NO UNIQUE SOLUTION"
220 GOTO 440
230 FOR K=1 TO R+1
240 X=A(J,K)
250 A(J,K)=A(I,K)
260 A(I,K)=X
270 NEXT K
280 Y=1/A(J,J)
290 FOR K=1 TO R+1
300 A(J,K)=Y*A(J,K)
310 NEXT K
320 FOR I=1 TO R
330 IF I=J THEN 380
340 Y=-A(I,J)
350 FOR K=1 TO R+1
360 A(I,K)=A(I,K)+Y*A(J,K)
370 NEXT K
380 NEXT I
390 NEXT J
400 PRINT
410 FOR I=1 TO R
420 PRINT "X";I;" = ";INT(A(I,R+1)*1000+0.5)/1000
430 NEXT I
440 END
```

Linear Programming

Courtesy: Harold Hanes
Earlham College
Richmond, Indiana

This program uses the simplex method to solve a linear programming problem. You must provide the coefficients of the objective function and the coefficients, relation, and constant of each constraint. This information is entered in DATA statements before you run the program.

After you load the program, enter the DATA statements according to the following instructions. If you run more than one problem, remember to clear out all DATA statements from the previous problem before running the new problem. Our DATA statements occur at lines 30 through 35.

1. Arrange your problem constraints according to their relation, so that the "less than" inequalities precede the equalities, which in turn precede the "greater than" inequalities.

2. Type in as DATA the coefficients of the constraints, in the order the constraints were arranged in step 1. Do not include coefficients for slack, surplus, or artificial variables. Do include a '0' coefficient for any variable that doesn't appear in a particular constraint.

3. Type in as DATA the constants of the constraints (right-hand sides of the constraints) in the same order as you entered the rows of coefficients. These values cannot be negative.

4. Type in as DATA the coefficients of the objective function.

You must select whether the problem solution is to be a minimum or maximum value. The program also asks you to enter the total number of constraints and the number of variables to allow for each, and the number of "less than," "equal," and "greater than" constraints you are considering.

The dimension statement at line 180 limits the number of variables and constraints you may enter. You can change these limits according to the following scheme:

$$180 \ \text{DIM} \ A(C+2, V+C+G+1), B(C+2)$$

where: C = number of constraints
V = number of variables
G = number of "greater than" constraints

Example:

A manufacturer wishes to produce 100 pounds of an alloy which is 83% lead, 14% iron, and 3% antimony. He has five available alloys with the following compositions and prices:

Alloy 1	Alloy 2	Alloy 3	Alloy 4	Alloy 5
90	80	95	70	30
5	5	2	30	70
5	15	3	0	0
$6.13	$7.12	$5.85	$4.57	$3.96

How should he combine these alloys to get the desired product at minimum cost?
Note that this problem results in the following system of equations:

$$
\begin{aligned}
x_1 + x_2 + x_3 + x_4 + x_5 &= 100 \\
0.90x_1 + 0.80x_2 + 0.95x_3 + 0.70x_4 + 0.30x_5 &= 83 \\
0.05x_1 + 0.05x_2 + 0.02x_3 + 0.30x_4 + 0.70x_5 &= 14 \\
0.05x_1 + 0.15x_2 + 0.03x_3 &= 3 \\
6.13x_1 + 7.12x_2 + 5.85x_3 + 4.57x_4 + 3.96x_5 &= Z \, (\text{min})
\end{aligned}
$$

LINEAR PROGRAMMING — SIMPLEX METHOD

```
1 MAXIMIZES -1 MINIMIZES? -1
# OF CONSTRAINTS,# OF VARIABLES
? 4,5
# OF <,=,> CONSTRAINTS? 0,4,0


YOUR VARIABLES 1 THROUGH 5
ARTIFICIAL VARIABLES 6 THROUGH 9

ANSWERS:
PRIMAL VARIABLES:
VARIABLES              VALUE
2          10.43478262
3          47.82608693
4          41.73913042
VALUE OF OBJECTIVE
FUNCTION =544.826087
```

```
5 GRAPHICS 0
20 REM - *** DO THE FOLLOWING STEPS BEFORE RUNNING THE PROGRAM ***
21 REM - TYPE IN COEFFICIENTS OF <<<,<=<,<>< CONSTRAINTS IN DATA STATE
MENTS;
22 REM - STARTING AT LINE 30, A SEPARATE DATA STATEMENT FOR EACH CON
STRAINT;
23 REM - (LINES 30-33 IN OUR EXAMPLE)
24 REM - TYPE IN CONSTANTS OF THE CONSTRAINTS IN A DATA STATEMENT FOL
LOWING
25 REM - THE COEFFICIENT DATA, AND IN THE SAME ORDER AS THE CONSTRAINT
DATA
26 REM - WERE ENTERED (LINE 34 IN OUR EXAMPLE)
27 REM - TYPE IN COEFFICIENTS OF THE OBJECTIVE FUNCTION IN A DATA STATE
MENT
28 REM - (LINE 35 IN OUR EXAMPLE) FOLLOWING THE CONSTANTS DATA
30 DATA 1,1,1,1,1
31 DATA .9,.8,.95,.7,.3
32 DATA .05,.05,.02,.3,.7
33 DATA .05,.15,.03,0,0
34 DATA 100,83,14,3
35 DATA 6.13,7.12,5.85,4.57,3.96
100 GRAPHICS 0
170 PRINT "LINEAR PROGRAMMING -- ";
175 PRINT "SIMPLEX METHOD"
180 DIM A(6,10),B(6)
200 PRINT
210 PRINT "1 MAXIMIZES -1 MINIMIZES";
220 INPUT Z
230 Z=-Z
240 PRINT "# OF CONSTRAINTS,# OF ";
245 PRINT "VARIABLES";
250 INPUT M,N
260 PRINT "# OF <,=,> CONSTRAINTS";
270 INPUT L,E,G
280 IF M=L+E+G THEN 320
290 PRINT "INCONSISTENT DATA - ";
```

```
295 PRINT "TRY AGAIN"
300 GOTO 260
319 REM - THIS IS THE INITIALIZATION ROUTINE
320 C=N+M+G
330 C1=C+1
340 C2=N+L+G
350 M1=M+1
360 M2=M+2
380 PRINT
390 FOR I=1 TO M2
400 FOR J=1 TO C1
410 A(I,J)=0
420 NEXT J
430 NEXT I
440 FOR I=1 TO M
450 B(I)=0
460 NEXT I
470 FOR I=1 TO M
480 FOR J=1 TO N
490 READ A1
492 A(I,J)=A1
500 IF I<=L THEN 520
510 A(M1,J)=A(M1,J)-A(I,J)
520 NEXT J
530 IF I>L THEN 570
540 B(I)=N+I
550 A(I,N+I)=1
560 GOTO 630
570 B(I)=N+G+I
580 A(I,N+G+I)=1
590 IF I>L+E THEN 610
600 GOTO 630
610 A(I,N+I-E)=-1
620 A(M1,N+I-E)=1
630 NEXT I
640 FOR I=1 TO M
650 READ A1
652 A(I,C1)=A1
660 NEXT I
670 FOR J=1 TO N
680 READ A1
682 A(M2,J)=A1
690 A(M2,J)=Z*A(M2,J)
700 NEXT J
710 PRINT
730 PRINT "YOUR VARIABLES ";
731 PRINT "1 THROUGH ";N
740 IF L=0 THEN 760
750 PRINT "SLACK VARIABLES ";
751 PRINT N+1;" THROUGH ";N+L
760 IF G=0 THEN 780
770 PRINT "SURPLUS VARIABLES ";
771 PRINT N+L+1;" THROUGH ";C2
780 IF L=M THEN 970
790 PRINT "ARTIFICIAL VARIABLES ";
```

```
791 PRINT C2+1;" THROUGH ";C
800 M3=M1
810 GOSUB 1240
820 PRINT
830 FOR I1=1 TO M
840 IF B(I1)<=C2 THEN 950
850 IF A(I1,C1)<=1.0E-05 THEN 880
860 PRINT "NO FEASIBLE SOLUTION"
870 GOTO 1700
880 FOR J1=1 TO C2
890 IF ABS(A(I1,J1))<=1.0E-05 THEN 940
900 R=I1
910 S=J1
920 GOSUB 1490
930 J1=C2
940 NEXT J1
950 NEXT I1
970 PRINT
980 M3=M2
990 GOSUB 1240
1020 PRINT
1030 PRINT "ANSWERS:"
1040 PRINT "PRIMAL VARIABLES:"
1050 PRINT "VARIABLES","VALUE"
1060 FOR J=1 TO C2
1070 FOR I=1 TO M
1080 IF B(I)<>J THEN 1110
1090 PRINT J,A(I,C1)
1100 I=M
1110 NEXT I
1120 NEXT J
1130 IF L=0 THEN 1190
1140 PRINT "DUAL VARIABLES:"
1150 PRINT "VARIABLE","VALUE"
1160 FOR I=1 TO L
1170 PRINT I,-Z*A(M2,N+I)
1180 NEXT I
1190 PRINT "VALUE OF OBJECTIVE"
1191 PRINT "FUNCTION =";-Z*A(M2,C1)
1200 PRINT
1210 PRINT
1220 PRINT
1230 GOTO 1700
1240 REM - OPTIMIZATION ROUTINE
1241 REM - FIRST PRICE OUT COLUMNS
1260 P=-1.0E-05
1270 FOR J=1 TO C2
1280 IF A(M3,J)>=P THEN 1310
1290 S=J
1300 P=A(M3,J)
1310 NEXT J
1320 IF P=-1.0E-05 THEN 1680
1330 GOSUB 1350
1340 GOSUB 1440
1345 GOTO 1260
```

```
1350 REM - NOW FIND WHICH VARIABLE LEAVE BASIS
1360 Q=1E+38
1370 FOR I=1 TO M
1380 IF A(I,S)<=1.0E-05 THEN 1420
1390 IF A(I,C1)/A(I,S)>=Q THEN 1420
1400 R=I
1410 Q=A(I,C1)/A(I,S)
1420 NEXT I
1430 RETURN
1440 IF Q=1E+38 THEN 1470
1450 GOSUB 1490
1460 RETURN
1470 PRINT "THE SOLUTION IS UNBOUNDED"
1480 GOTO 1700
1490 REM - PERFORM PIVOTING
1500 P=A(R,S)
1510 FOR I=1 TO M2
1520 IF I=R THEN 1590
1530 FOR J=1 TO C1
1540 IF J=S THEN 1580
1550 A(I,J)=A(I,J)-A(I,S)*A(R,J)/P
1560 IF ABS(A(I,J))>=1.0E-05 THEN 1580
1570 A(I,J)=0
1580 NEXT J
1590 NEXT I
1600 FOR J=1 TO C1
1610 A(R,J)=A(R,J)/P
1620 NEXT J
1630 FOR I=1 TO M2
1640 A(I,S)=0
1650 NEXT I
1660 A(R,S)=1
1670 B(R)=S
1680 RETURN
1700 END
```

Matrix Addition, Subtraction, Scalar Multiplication

This program adds or subtracts two matrices, or multiplies a matrix by a given scalar. You must input the value of each element of each matrix. To perform addition or subtraction the dimensions of the two matrices must be equal.

The dimension of the matrices may be increased or decreased depending on the amount of memory available in your system. Statement 30 may be changed to:

$$30 \ \text{DIM} \ A(X, Y), \ B(X, Y)$$

where (X, Y) is your limit on the dimension of the matrices.

Example:

Find the sum of the following matrices, then multiply the resultant matrix by 3.

$$\begin{bmatrix} 1 & 0 & -1 \\ 5 & 8 & 0.5 \\ -1 & 2 & 0 \end{bmatrix} \qquad \begin{bmatrix} -5 & -1 & 2 \\ 6 & -0.1 & 0 \\ 3 & 4 & -2 \end{bmatrix}$$

```
MATRIX ADDITION, SUBTRACTION,
SCALAR MULTIPLICATION

1=ADDITION
2=SUBTRACTION
3=SCALAR MULTIPLICATION

WHICH OPERATION? 1
DIMENSION OF MATRIX (R,C)? 3,3
MATRIX 1:
ROW 1
VALUE COLUMN 1? 1
VALUE COLUMN 2? 0
VALUE COLUMN 3? -1
ROW 2
VALUE COLUMN 1? 5
VALUE COLUMN 2? 8
VALUE COLUMN 3? 0.5
ROW 3
VALUE COLUMN 1? -1
VALUE COLUMN 2? 2
VALUE COLUMN 3? 0
MATRIX 2:
ROW 1
VALUE COLUMN 1? -5
VALUE COLUMN 2? -1
VALUE COLUMN 3? 2
ROW 2
VALUE COLUMN 1? 6
```

```
VALUE COLUMN 2? -0.1
VALUE COLUMN 3? 0
ROW 3
VALUE COLUMN 1? 3
VALUE COLUMN 2? 4
VALUE COLUMN 3? -2
-4   -1   1
11   7.9   0.5
2   6   -2

MORE DATA? (1=YES, 0=NO)? 1
1=ADDITION
2=SUBTRACTION
3=SCALAR MULTIPLICATION

WHICH OPERATION? 3
VALUE OF SCALAR? 3
DIMENSION OF MATRIX (R,C)? 3,3
MATRIX 1:
ROW 1
VALUE COLUMN 1? -4
VALUE COLUMN 2? -1
VALUE COLUMN 3? 1
ROW 2
VALUE COLUMN 1? 11
VALUE COLUMN 2? 7.9
VALUE COLUMN 3? 0.5
ROW 3
VALUE COLUMN 1? 2
VALUE COLUMN 2? 6
VALUE COLUMN 3? -2
-12   -3   3
33   23.7   1.5
6   18   -6

MORE DATA? (1=YES, 0=NO)? 0

5 GRAPHICS 0
20 PRINT "MATRIX ADDITION, ";
21 PRINT "SUBTRACTION,"
22 PRINT "SCALAR MULTIPLICATION"
25 PRINT
29 REM - ARRAYS SHOULD BE SET TO DIMENSONS OF MATRICES
30 DIM A(3,3),B(3,3)
40 PRINT "1=ADDITION"
50 PRINT "2=SUBTRACTION"
60 PRINT "3=SCALAR MULTIPLICATION"
65 PRINT
69 REM - SELECT OPERATION BY ENTERING THE OPERATION NUMBER (1-3)
70 PRINT "WHICH OPERATION";
80 INPUT D
89 REM - TEST FOR ADDITION OR SUBTRACTION
90 IF D<>3 THEN 120
100 PRINT "VALUE OF SCALAR";
110 INPUT S
```

```
120 PRINT "DIMENSION OF MATRIX (R,C)";
130 INPUT R,C
138 REM - LOOP TO ENTER MATRIX VALUES
139 REM - FOR SUBTRACTION, MATRIX 2 SUBTRACTED FROM MATRIX 1
140 FOR K=1 TO 2
150 IF K=2 THEN 180
160 PRINT "MATRIX 1:"
170 GOTO 190
180 PRINT "MATRIX 2:"
190 FOR J=1 TO R
200 PRINT "ROW ";J
210 FOR I=1 TO C
220 PRINT "VALUE COLUMN ";I;
230 IF K=2 THEN 260
240 INPUT A1
242 A(J,I)=A1
250 GOTO 270
260 INPUT B1
262 B(J,I)=B1
270 NEXT I
280 NEXT J
289 REM - ONLY ONE MATRIX USED FOR SCALAR MULTIPLICATION
290 IF D=3 THEN 310
300 NEXT K
308 REM - STATEMENTS 310 TO 410 PERFORM REQUESTED OPERATION AND PRINT
309 REM - RESULTANT MATRIX
310 FOR J=1 TO R
320 FOR I=1 TO C
330 IF D<>2 THEN 350
340 B(J,I)=-B(J,I)
350 IF D=3 THEN 380
360 PRINT A(J,I)+B(J,I);"   ";
370 GOTO 390
380 PRINT A(J,I)*S;"   ";
390 NEXT I
399 REM - ADVANCE OUTPUT DEVICE TO PRINT NEXT ROW
400 PRINT
410 NEXT J
420 PRINT
429 REM - RESTART OR END PROGRAM? USER INPUT REQUIRED
430 PRINT "MORE DATA? (1=YES, 0=NO)";
440 INPUT D
450 IF D=1 THEN 40
460 END
```

Matrix Multiplication

This program multiplies two matrices. The first matrix is multiplied by the second. You must input the elements of each matrix.

The dimensions of the matrices are presently limited to 20 × 20. This limit may be increased or decreased by altering line 10 according to the following scheme:

$$10 \text{ DIM } A(X, Y), \ B(Z, X)$$

where: (X, Y) = dimension of matrix 1
(Z, X) = dimension of matrix 2

Example:

Multiply matrix 1 by matrix 2.

$$
1 \begin{cases}
2 & -1 & 4 & 1 & 2 \\
1 & 0 & 1 & 2 & -1 \\
2 & 3 & -1 & 0 & -2
\end{cases}
$$

$$
2 \begin{cases}
-2 & -1 & 2 \\
0 & 2 & 1 \\
-1 & 1 & 4 \\
3 & 0 & -1 \\
2 & 1 & 2
\end{cases}
$$

```
MATRIX MULTIPLICATION

MATRIX 1 DIMENSION (R,C)? 3,5
MATRIX 2 DIMENSION (R,C)? 5,3
MATRIX 1:
ROW 1
VALUE COLUMN 1? 2
VALUE COLUMN 2? -1
VALUE COLUMN 3? 4
VALUE COLUMN 4? 1
VALUE COLUMN 5? 2
ROW 2
VALUE COLUMN 1? 1
VALUE COLUMN 2? 0
VALUE COLUMN 3? 1
VALUE COLUMN 4? 2
VALUE COLUMN 5? -1
ROW 3
VALUE COLUMN 1? 2
VALUE COLUMN 2? 3
VALUE COLUMN 3? -1
VALUE COLUMN 4? 0
VALUE COLUMN 5? -2
```

```
MATRIX 2:
ROW 1
VALUE COLUMN 1? -2
VALUE COLUMN 2? -1
VALUE COLUMN 3? 2
ROW 2
VALUE COLUMN 1? O
VALUE COLUMN 2? 2
VALUE COLUMN 3? 1
ROW 3
VALUE COLUMN 1? -1
VALUE COLUMN 2? 1
VALUE COLUMN 3? 4
ROW 4
VALUE COLUMN 1? 3
VALUE COLUMN 2? O
VALUE COLUMN 3? -1
ROW 5
VALUE COLUMN 1? 2
VALUE COLUMN 2? 1
VALUE COLUMN 3? 2


-1   2   22
 1  -1   2
-7   1  -1
```

```
5 GRAPHICS O
9 REM - ARRAYS A AND B SHOULD BE SET TO DIMENSIONS OF MATRICES
10 DIM A(20,20),B(20,20)
20 PRINT "MATRIX MULTIPLICATION"
30 PRINT
40 PRINT "MATRIX 1 DIMENSION (R,C)";
50 INPUT R1,C1
60 PRINT "MATRIX 2 DIMENSION (R,C)";
70 INPUT R2,C2
79 REM - # OF COLUMNS IN MATRIX 1 MUST EQUAL # OF ROWS IN MATRIX 2
80 IF C1=R2 THEN 110
90 PRINT "CANNOT BE MULTIPLIED"
100 GOTO 40
109 REM - ENTER MATRIX VALUES
110 PRINT "MATRIX 1:"
120 FOR J=1 TO R1
130 PRINT "ROW ";J
140 FOR I=1 TO C1
150 PRINT "VALUE COLUMN ";I;
160 INPUT X
162 A(J,I)=X
170 NEXT I
180 NEXT J
190 PRINT
200 PRINT "MATRIX 2:"
210 FOR J=1 TO R2
220 PRINT "ROW ";J
230 FOR I=1 TO C2
240 PRINT "VALUE COLUMN ";I;
```

```
250  INPUT X
252  B(J,I)=X
260  NEXT I
270  NEXT J
280  PRINT
289  REM - PERFORM MATRIX MULTIPLICATION, PRINT RESULTANT MATRIX
290  FOR I=1 TO R1
300  FOR J=1 TO C2
310  S=0
320  FOR K=1 TO C1
330  S=S+A(I,K)*B(K,J)
340  NEXT K
350  PRINT S;"   ";
360  NEXT J
369  REM - ADVANCE OUTPUT DEVICE TO PRINT NEXT ROW
370  PRINT
380  NEXT I
390  END
```

Matrix Inversion

This program inverts a square matrix. The inversion is performed by a modified Gauss-Jordan elimination method.

The dimensions of the matrices are presently limited to 20 × 20. This limit may be increased or decreased by altering line 30 according to the following scheme:

$$30 \; \text{DIM} \; A(R, R), \; B(R, R)$$

where R = number of rows (or columns) in the matrix.

Example:

Invert matrix A.

$$A \begin{cases} 3 & 5 & -1 & -4 \\ 1 & 4 & -0.7 & -3 \\ 0 & -2 & 0 & 1 \\ -2 & 6 & 0 & 0.3 \end{cases}$$

```
MATRIX INVERSION

MATRIX DIMENSION? 4
MATRIX ELEMENTS:
ROW 1
VALUE COLUMN 1? 3
VALUE COLUMN 2? 5
VALUE COLUMN 3? -1
VALUE COLUMN 4? -4
ROW 2
VALUE COLUMN 1? 1
VALUE COLUMN 2? 4
VALUE COLUMN 3? -0.7
VALUE COLUMN 4? -3
ROW 3
VALUE COLUMN 1? 0
VALUE COLUMN 2? -2
VALUE COLUMN 3? 0
VALUE COLUMN 4? 1
ROW 4
VALUE COLUMN 1? -2
VALUE COLUMN 2? 6
VALUE COLUMN 3? 0
VALUE COLUMN 4? 0.3

0.654   -0.935   -0.191   0.014
0.198   -0.283   -0.103   0.156
0.368   -1.955   -4.263   -0.425
0.397   -0.567   0.793    0.312

5 GRAPHICS 0
10 PRINT "MATRIX INVERSION"
20 PRINT
29 REM - A() AND B() SHOULD BOTH BE SET TO THE DIMENSIONS OF THE MATRIX
30 DIM A(20,20),B(20,20)
```

```
39 REM - MATRIX IS SQUARE SO ONLY ONE DIMENSION IS NEEDED
40 PRINT "MATRIX DIMENSION";
50 INPUT R
60 PRINT "MATRIX ELEMENTS:"
69 REM - ENTER MATRIX ELEMENTS
70 FOR J=1 TO R
80 PRINT "ROW ";J
90 FOR I=1 TO R
100 PRINT "VALUE COLUMN ";I;
110 INPUT A1
112 A(J,I)=A1
114 B(J,I)=0
120 NEXT I
130 B(J,J)=1
140 NEXT J
149 REM - STATEMENTS 150 TO 420 INVERT MATRIX
150 FOR J=1 TO R
160 FOR I=J TO R
170 IF A(I,J)<>0 THEN 210
180 NEXT I
190 PRINT "SINGULAR MATRIX"
200 GOTO 500
210 FOR K=1 TO R
220 S=A(J,K)
230 A(J,K)=A(I,K)
240 A(I,K)=S
250 S=B(J,K)
260 B(J,K)=B(I,K)
270 B(I,K)=S
280 NEXT K
290 T=1/A(J,J)
300 FOR K=1 TO R
310 A(J,K)=T*A(J,K)
320 B(J,K)=T*B(J,K)
330 NEXT K
340 FOR L=1 TO R
350 IF L=J THEN 410
360 T=-1*A(L,J)
370 FOR K=1 TO R
380 A(L,K)=A(L,K)+T*A(J,K)
390 B(L,K)=B(L,K)+T*B(J,K)
400 NEXT K
410 NEXT L
420 NEXT J
430 PRINT
439 REM - PRINT RESULTANT MATRIX
440 FOR I=1 TO R
450 FOR J=1 TO R
459 REM - ROUND OFF, PRINT
460 PRINT INT(B(I,J)*1000+0.5)/1000;
461 PRINT "   ";
470 NEXT J
479 REM - ADVANCE OUTPUT DEVICE TO PRINT NEXT LINE
480 PRINT
490 NEXT I
500 END
```

Permutations and Combinations

This program computes the number of permutations and combinations of *N* objects taken *D* at a time.

Examples:

How many permutations and combinations can be made of the 26 letters of the alphabet, taking 5 at a time?

How many different ways can 12 people sit on a bench if there is only room for 2 at a time?

```
PERMUTATIONS & COMBINATIONS

(ENTER 0 TO END PROGRAM)
TOTAL NUMBER OF OBJECTS? 26
SIZE OF SUBGROUP? 5
7893600 PERMUTATIONS
65780 COMBINATIONS

TOTAL NUMBER OF OBJECTS? 12
SIZE OF SUBGROUP? 2
132 PERMUTATIONS
66 COMBINATIONS

TOTAL NUMBER OF OBJECTS? 0

10 GRAPHICS 0
20 PRINT "PERMUTATIONS & COMBINATIONS"
25 PRINT
30 PRINT "(ENTER 0 TO END PROGRAM)"
40 PRINT "TOTAL NUMBER OF OBJECTS";
50 INPUT N
59 REM - TEST FOR END OF PROGRAM
60 IF N=0 THEN 280
70 PRINT "SIZE OF SUBGROUP";
80 INPUT D
89 REM - SIZE OF SUBGROUP CANNOT BE LARGER THAN SIZE OF GROUP
90 IF D<=N THEN 130
100 PRINT "SUBGROUP TOO LARGE"
110 PRINT
120 GOTO 40
129 REM - LINES 130 TO 200 COMPUTE PERMUTATIONS
130 P=1
140 C=1
150 FOR I=N-D+1 TO N
159 REM - DON'T ALLOW NUMBER SIZE TO OVERFLOW MACHINE CAPACITY
160 IF 1.7E+97/I>=P THEN 190
170 PRINT "> 1.7E97 PERMUTATIONS"
180 GOTO 280
190 P=P*I
200 NEXT I
```

```
209 REM - COMPUTE INTERMEDIATE FACTORIAL FOR COMBINATIONS
210 FOR J=2 TO D
220 C=C*J
230 NEXT J
240 PRINT P;" PERMUTATIONS"
250 PRINT P/C;" COMBINATIONS"
260 PRINT
269 REM - RESTART PROGRAM
270 GOTO 40
280 END
```

Mann-Whitney *U* Test

This program performs the Mann-Whitney *U* test on samples from two populations.

The dimension statement at line 30 limits the size of the samples. You can increase or decrease the dimension limits according to the following scheme:

$$30 \ \text{DIM} \ X(M), Y(N)$$

where: M = maximum size of first sample
N = maximum size of second sample

Example:

A group of ten women and a group of ten men were asked to rate the flavor of a frozen T.V. dinner on a scale of one to ten. The table below lists the scores. Count the number of times the women's scores are lower than the men's, and vice versa.

Women	1	3	4	3	6	8	9	7	8	4
Men	7	9	8	5	10	9	10	6	5	2

```
MANN-WHITNEY U-TEST

SAMPLE 1:
  SIZE? 10
    DATA 1? 1
    DATA 2? 3
    DATA 3? 4
    DATA 4? 3
    DATA 5? 6
    DATA 6? 8
    DATA 7? 9
    DATA 8? 7
    DATA 9? 8
    DATA 10? 4

SAMPLE 2:
  SIZE? 10
    DATA 1? 7
    DATA 2? 9
    DATA 3? 8
    DATA 4? 5
    DATA 5? 10
    DATA 6? 9
    DATA 7? 10
    DATA 8? 6
    DATA 9? 5
    DATA 10? 2

FIRST PRECEDING, U = 71.5
SECOND PRECEDING, U = 28.5
```

```
5 GRAPHICS O
10 PRINT "MANN-WHITNEY U-TEST"
20 PRINT
28 REM - SET MAXIMUM SAMPLE SIZE TO X(M),Y(N) (WHERE M=MAXIMUM SIZE OF;
29 REM - SAMPLE 1, N=MAXIMUM SIZE OF SAMPLE 2)
30 DIM X(25),Y(25)
40 DIM N(2)
49 REM - INPUT THE TWO SAMPLES
50 FOR I=1 TO 2
60 PRINT "SAMPLE ";I;":"
70 PRINT "  SIZE";
80 INPUT A
82 N(I)=A
90 FOR J=1 TO N(I)
100 PRINT "   DATA ";J;
110 INPUT A
112 Y(J)=A
120 NEXT J
129 REM - SORT EACH SAMPLE
130 FOR J=1 TO N(I)
140 FOR K=1 TO N(I)-J
150 C=Y(K)
170 IF Y(K)<Y(K+1) THEN 200
180 Y(K)=Y(K+1)
190 Y(K+1)=C
200 NEXT K
210 NEXT J
220 PRINT
229 REM - TRANSFER FIRST EXAMPLE TO X-ARRAY
230 IF I=2 THEN 270
240 FOR J=1 TO N(1)
250 X(J)=Y(J)
260 NEXT J
270 NEXT I
279 REM - ADD UP RANKS
280 R=1
290 I=0
300 J=0
310 I=I+1
320 J=J+1
330 IF I>N(1) THEN 580
340 IF J>N(2) THEN 620
350 IF X(I)<Y(J) THEN 620
360 IF Y(J)<X(I) THEN 590
369 REM - LINES 370 TO 570 HANDLE EQUAL SCORES FROM BOTH SAMPLES
370 K=2
380 M=I
390 L=J
400 R1=2*R+1
410 R=R+2
420 I=I+1
430 J=J+1
440 IF I>N(1) THEN 480
450 IF X(I)<>(I-1) THEN 480
460 I=I+1
```

```
470 GOTO 510
480 IF J>N(2) THEN 550
490 IF Y(J)<>(J-1) THEN 550
500 J=J+1
510 R1=R1+R
520 R=R+1
530 K=K+1
540 GOTO 440
550 X=X+(I-M)*R1/K
560 Y=Y+(J-L)*R1/K
570 GOTO 330
580 IF J>N(2) THEN 660
590 Y=Y+R
600 J=J+1
610 GOTO 640
620 X=X+R
630 I=I+1
640 R=R+1
650 GOTO 330
659 REM - U1=NUMBER OF TIMES SAMPLE 1 SCORES PRECEDE SAMPLE 2 SCORES
660 U1=N(1)*N(2)+N(1)*(N(1)+1)/2--X
669 REM - U2=NUMBER OF TIMES SAMPLE 2 SCORES PRECEDE SAMPLE 1 SCORES
670 U2=N(1)*N(2)+N(2)*(N(2)+1)/2--Y
680 PRINT
690 PRINT "FIRST PRECEDING, U = ";U1
700 PRINT "SECOND PRECEDING, U = ";U2
710 END
```

```
30  PRINT "(TO END PROGRAM ENTER 0)"
40  PRINT "DEGREES OF FREEDOM";
50  INPUT V
60  IF V=0 THEN 280
70  PRINT "CHI-SQUARE";
80  INPUT W
89  REM - R=DENOMINATOR PRODUCT
90  R=1
100 FOR I=V TO 2 STEP -2
110 R=R*I
120 NEXT I
129 REM - K=THE NUMERATOR PRODUCT
130 K=W^(INT((V+1)/2))*EXP(-W/2)/R
139 REM - THE PI FACTOR IS USED ONLY WHEN DEGREES OF FREEDOM ARE ODD
140 IF INT(V/2)=V/2 THEN 170
150 J=SQR(2/W/PI)
160 GOTO 180
169 REM - L (SUMMATION FACTOR) CALCULATED LINES 170-240
170 J=1
180 L=1
190 M=1
200 V=V+2
210 M=M*W/V
219 REM - CHECK FOR END OF SUMMATION
220 IF M<1.0E-07 THEN 250
230 L=L+M
240 GOTO 200
250 PRINT "TAIL END VALUE =";1-J*K*L
260 PRINT
269 REM - RESTART PROGRAM
270 GOTO 40
280 END
```

OPTION

You may wish to compute the percentile rather than the tail-end value. This value corresponds to the unshaded area in the figure above. The program changes necessary are listed following the example below.

Example:

What is the percentile in the example above?

```
CHI-SQUARE DISTRIBUTION

(TO END PROGRAM ENTER 0)
DEGREES OF FREEDOM? 1
CHI-SQUARE? 2.571108
PERCENTILE = 0.8911685

DEGREES OF FREEDOM? 0
```

```
1 REM - OPTION 250
5 GRAPHICS 0
6 PI=3.14159265
10 PRINT "CHI-SQUARE DISTRIBUTION"
  .
  .
240 GOTO 200
250 PRINT "PERCENTILE = ";J*K*L
260 PRINT
269 REM - RESTART PROGRAM
270 GOTO 40
280 END
```

Chi-Square Test

This program calculates the chi-square (X^2) statistic and degrees of freedom associated with a given contingency table. The expected value for each cell and X^2 contribution from each cell are also printed.

The dimension statement at line 30 limits the size of the contingency table. You can change the dimensions according to the following scheme:

```
30 DIM V1(R·C),V2(C),A(R)
```

where: R = number of rows in the contingency table
C = number of columns in the contingency table

Example:

Of a group of people who complained they could not sleep well, some were given sleeping pills while others were given placebos. Later they were asked whether or not the pills had helped them sleep. The results are detailed in the table below. What is the value of the X^2 statistic?

	Slept Well	Slept Poorly
Sleeping pill	44	10
Placebo	81	35

```
CHI-SQUARE TEST

NUMBER OF ROWS? 2
NUMBER OF COLUMNS? 2
CONTINGENCY TABLE:
ROW 1
     ELEMENT 1? 44
     ELEMENT 2? 10
ROW 2
     ELEMENT 1? 81
     ELEMENT 2? 35

       OBSERVED              EXPECTED          CHI^2 CONTRIBUTION

       COLUMN 1
         44                39.70588235          0.3625490065
         81                85.29411764          0.1687728133
       COLUMN 2
         10                14.29411764          1.00708057
         35                30.70588235          0.4688133705


       CHI-SQUARE = 2.00721575
       DEGREES OF FREEDOM = 1


5 GRAPHICS 0
10 PRINT "CHI-SQUARE TEST"
20 PRINT
26 REM - LIMIT SIZE OF CONTINGENCY
27 REM - TABLES TO V1(R*C),V2(C),A(R)
```

```
28 REM - WHERE R=NUMBER OF ROWS,
29 REM - C=NUMBER OF COLUMNS
30 DIM V1(4),V2(2),A(2)
40 PRINT "NUMBER OF ROWS";
48 REM - INPUT CONTINGENCY TABLE
49 REM - LINES 50 TO 150
50 INPUT R
60 PRINT "NUMBER OF COLUMNS";
70 INPUT C
80 PRINT "CONTINGENCY TABLE:"
90 FOR I=1 TO R
100 PRINT "ROW ";I
110 FOR J=1 TO C
120 PRINT "    ELEMENT ";J;
130 INPUT X
132 V1((I-1)*C+J)=X
140 NEXT J
150 NEXT I
160 PRINT
168 REM - ADD UP MARGINAL FREQUENCIES
169 REM - FOR EACH ROW
170 L=0
180 M=1
190 FOR I=1 TO R
195 A(I)=0
200 FOR J=1 TO C
210 A(I)=A(I)+V1(M)
220 M=M+1
230 NEXT J
240 L=L+A(I)
250 NEXT I
260 N=R*C
268 REM - ADD UP MARGINAL FREQUENCIES
269 REM - FOR EACH COLUMN
270 FOR I=1 TO C
275 V2(I)=0
280 FOR J=I TO N STEP C
290 V2(I)=V2(I)+V1(J)
300 NEXT J
310 NEXT I
320 Z=0
330 PRINT "OBSERVED  EXPECTED  ";
331 PRINT "CHI^2 CONTRIBUTION"
340 FOR I=1 TO C
350 PRINT " COLUMN ";I
360 FOR J=1 TO R
369 REM - P=EXPECTED CELL VALUE
370 P=A(J)*V2(I)/L
375 X=I+(J-1)*C
377 REM - USE YATES' CORRECTION FOR
378 REM - CONTINUITY IN 2 X 2 CHI-
379 REM - SQUARE TEST
380 IF R<>2 THEN 390
381 IF C<>2 THEN 390
382 Y=(ABS(V1(X)-P)-0.5)^2/P
```

```
383  GOTO 400
388  REM - Y=CHI-SQUARE CONTRIBUTION
389  REM - FROM THIS CELL
390  Y=(V1(X)-P)^2/P
399  REM - Z=TOTAL CHI-SQUARE VALUE
400  Z=Z+Y
410  PRINT "    ";V1(X);"     ";P;
411  PRINT "    ";Y
420  NEXT J
430  NEXT I
440  PRINT
450  PRINT "CHI-SQUARE = ";Z
460  PRINT "DEGREES OF FREEDOM = ";
461  PRINT (C-1)*(R-1)
470  END
```

Student's *t*-distribution

This program calculates right-tail values for points on a *t*-distribution curve. You must provide the value of *t* and the degrees of freedom.

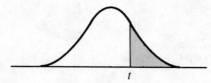

Student's *t*-distribution

The shaded area represents the right-tail value for *t*.

The right-tail value is approximated using the following formula:

$$\text{right-tail value} = \frac{1}{4}(1 + a_1 x + a_2 x^2 + a_3 x^3 + a_4 x^4)^{-4} + \epsilon(x)$$

where: $a_1 = 0.196854$
$a_2 = 0.115194$
$a_3 = 0.000344$
$a_4 = 0.019527$

$$x = \left(t^{2/3}\left(1 - \frac{2}{9d}\right) - \frac{7}{9}\right)\left(\frac{2}{9} + t^{1/3} \cdot \frac{2}{9d}\right)^{-1/2}$$

$$|\epsilon(x)| < 2.5 \cdot 10^{-4}$$

Examples:

What is the right-tail value when the *t*-value is 2.921 and there are 16 degrees of freedom?
   What is the right-tail value when the *t*-value is 11.178 and there are 5 degrees of freedom?

```
STUDENT'S T-DISTRIBUTION

(TO END PROGRAM ENTER 0)
T VALUE? 2.921
DEGREES OF FREEDOM? 16
RIGHT TAIL VALUE = 4.87140558E-03

T VALUE? 11.178
DEGREES OF FREEDOM? 5
RIGHT TAIL VALUE = 2.07763234E-04

T VALUE? 0


5 GRAPHICS 0
10 PRINT "STUDENT'S T-DISTRIBUTION"
20 PRINT
30 PRINT "(TO END PROGRAM ENTER 0)"
40 PRINT "T VALUE";
```

```
50  INPUT T
60  IF T=0 THEN 340
70  PRINT "DEGREES OF FREEDOM";
80  INPUT D
90  X=1
100  Y=1
110  T=T^2
119  REM - COMPUTE USING INVERSE FOR SMALL VALUES
120  IF T<1 THEN 170
130  S=Y
140  R=D
150  Z=T
160  GOTO 200
170  S=D
180  R=Y
190  Z=1/T
200  J=2/9/S
210  K=2/9/R
219  REM - COMPUTE USING APPROXIMATION FORMULAS
220  L=ABS((1-K)*Z^(1/3)-1+J)/SQR(K*Z^(2/3)+J)
230  IF R<4 THEN 270
240  X=0.25/(1+L*(0.196854+L*(0.115194+L*(3.44E-04+L*0.019527))))^4
260  GOTO 290
270  L=L*(1+0.08*L^4/R^3)
280  GOTO 240
289  REM - ADJUST IF INVERSE WAS COMPUTED
290  IF T>=1 THEN 310
300  X=1-X
310  PRINT "RIGHT TAIL VALUE = ";X
320  PRINT
330  GOTO 40
340  END
```

Student's *t*-distribution Test

This program calculates the *t*-statistic and degrees of freedom for Student's *t* Distribution. The calculations can be based on any one of three hypotheses.

The first hypothesis assumes that one population mean is equal to a given value. You must enter the elements of the sample and the value of the mean.

The remaining hypotheses compare two populations. In both tests the means of the two populations are equal, but the standard deviations may be equal or unequal. For these hypotheses you must enter the elements of each sample.

The dimension statement at line 30 limits the size of the samples you may enter. You can change the limit according to the following scheme:

$$30 \text{ DIM } P(N,2)$$

where N = maximum sample size.

Examples:

A sample of children's IQs was taken, the results being 101, 99, 120, 79, 111, 98, 106, 112, 87, and 97. Calculate the *t*-statistic assuming the population mean is 100.

A second sample was taken, the results being 101, 95, 130, 150, 75, 79, 111, 100, 98, and 91. Calculate the *t*-statistic based on the hypothesis that the two samples have equal means and standard deviations.

```
STUDENT'S T-DISTRIBUTION TEST

TEST 1: MEAN = X
TEST 2: MEAN = MEAN,SD = SD
TEST 3: MEAN = MEAN,SD <> SD

WHICH HYPOTHESIS? 1

SAMPLE 1 :
 NUMBER OF ELEMENTS? 10
  ELEMENT 1? 101
  ELEMENT 2? 99
  ELEMENT 3? 120
  ELEMENT 4? 79
  ELEMENT 5? 111
  ELEMENT 6? 98
  ELEMENT 7? 106
  ELEMENT 8? 112
  ELEMENT 9? 87
  ELEMENT 10? 97

VALUE OF MEAN? 100

T-VALUE = 0.2615130568
DEGREES OF FREEDOM = 9
```

```
5 GRAPHICS O
10 PRINT "STUDENT'S T-DISTRIBUTION TEST"
20 PRINT
28 REM - LIMIT SAMPLE SIZE TO P(N,2)
29 REM - WHERE N=MAXIMUM SAMPLE SIZE
30 DIM P(10,2)
40 DIM V(2),R(2),M(2),D(2)
50 PRINT "TEST 1: MEAN = X"
60 PRINT "TEST 2: MEAN = MEAN,SD = SD"
70 PRINT "TEST 3: MEAN = MEAN,SD <> SD"
80 PRINT
85 PRINT "WHICH HYPOTHESIS";
90 INPUT T
100 PRINT
108 REM - INPUT 1 OR 2 SAMPLES
109 REM - DEPENDING ON HYPOTHESIS
110 FOR I=1 TO SGN(T-1)+1
120 V(I)=0
130 D(I)=0
140 PRINT "SAMPLE ";I;" :"
150 PRINT " NUMBER OF ELEMENTS";
160 INPUT X
162 R(I)=X
170 FOR J=1 TO R(I)
180 PRINT "   ELEMENT ";J;
190 INPUT X
192 P(J,I)=X
199 REM - ACCUMULATE SAMPLES
200 V(I)=V(I)+P(J,I)
210 D(I)=D(I)+P(J,I)^2
220 NEXT J
229 REM - COMPUTE INTERMEDIATE VALUES
230 M(I)=V(I)/R(I)
240 V(I)=(D(I)-V(I)^2/R(I))/(R(I)-1)
250 NEXT I
260 PRINT
270 IF T=2 THEN 340
280 IF T=3 THEN 380
289 REM - INPUT GIVEN VALUE FOR FIRST HYPOTHESIS
290 PRINT "VALUE OF MEAN";
300 INPUT M
309 REM - COMPUTE T AND DEGREES OF FREEDOM FOR FIRST HYPOTHESIS
310 A=(M(1)-M)*SQR(R(1)/V(1))
320 B=R(1)-1
330 GOTO 420
339 REM - COMPUTE T AND DEGREES OF FREEDOM FOR SECOND HYPOTHESIS
340 A=(M(1)-M(2))/SQR(1/R(1)+1/R(2))
350 B=R(1)+R(2)-2
360 A=A/SQR(((R(1)-1)*V(1)+(R(2)-1)*V(2))/B)
370 GOTO 420
390 B=(V(1)/R(1)+V(2)/R(2))^2
410 B=INT(B+0.5)
420 PRINT
430 PRINT "T-VALUE = ";ABS(A)
440 PRINT "DEGREES OF FREEDOM = ";B
450 END
```

F-distribution

This program calculates percentile values for given values on an F-distribution curve. You must provide the value of F, the degrees of freedom in the numerator and the degrees of freedom in the denominator.

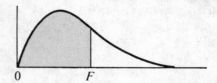

The F-distribution

The area of the shaded region represents the percentile.

The F-distribution function is approximated using the following formula:

$$\text{percentile} = 1 - \frac{1}{2}(1 + a_1 y + a_2 y^2 + a_3 y^3 + a_4 y^4)^{-4} + \epsilon(y)$$

where: $a_1 = 0.196854$
$a_2 = 0.115194$
$a_3 = 0.000344$
$a_4 = 0.019527$

$$y = \left(F^{1/3}\left(1 - \frac{2}{9d_2}\right) - \left(1 - \frac{2}{9d_1}\right)\right)\left(\frac{2}{9d_1} + F^{2/3} \cdot \frac{2}{9d_2}\right)^{-1/2}$$

$d_1 = $ degrees of freedom in numerator
$d_2 = $ degrees of freedom in denominator

$$|\epsilon(y)| < 2.5 \cdot 10^{-4}$$

Examples:

What is the percentile on an F-distribution curve when the F-value is 0.474 and the degrees of freedom are 1 and 18?
What is the percentile when the F-value is 23.7 and the degrees of freedom are 3 and 6?

```
F-DISTRIBUTION

(TO END PROGRAM ENTER 0)
F-VALUE? 0.474
DEGREES OF FREEDOM IN NUMERATOR? 1
DEGREES OF FREEDOM IN DENOMINATOR? 18
PERCENTILE = 0.4937

F-VALUE? 23.7
DEGREES OF FREEDOM IN NUMERATOR? 3
DEGREES OF FREEDOM IN DENOMINATOR? 6
PERCENTILE = 0.9984

F-VALUE? 0
```

```
5 GRAPHICS O
10 PRINT "F-DISTRIBUTION"
20 PRINT
30 PRINT "(TO END PROGRAM ENTER O)"
40 PRINT "F-VALUE";
50 INPUT F
60 IF F=O THEN 340
70 PRINT "DEGREES OF FREEDOM IN NUMERATOR";
80 INPUT D1
90 PRINT "DEGREES OF FREEDOM IN DENOMINATOR";
100 INPUT D2
110 X=1
119 REM - COMPUTE USING INVERSE FOR SMALL F-VALUES
120 IF F<1 THEN 170
130 S=D1
140 T=D2
150 Z=F
160 GOTO 200
170 S=D2
180 T=D1
190 Z=1/F
200 J=2/9/S
210 K=2/9/T
219 REM - COMPUTE USING APPROXIMATION FORMULAS
220 Y=ABS((1-K)*Z^(1/3)-1+J)/SQR(K*Z^(2/3)+J)
230 IF T<4 THEN 270
240 X=0.5/(1+Y*(0.196854+Y*(0.115194+Y*(3.44E-04+Y*0.019527))))^4
250 X=INT(X*10000+0.5)/10000
260 GOTO 290
270 Y=Y*(1+0.08*Y^4/T^3)
280 GOTO 240
289 REM - ADJUST IF INVERSE WAS COMPUTED
290 IF F>=1 THEN 310
300 X=1-X
310 PRINT "PERCENTILE = ";1-X
320 PRINT
329 REM - RESTART PROGRAM
330 GOTO 40
340 END
```

OPTION

You may prefer to compute the tail-end value (the area of the unshaded region in the figure above). The necessary program changes are listed following the examples below.

Examples:

What is the tail-end value on an *F*-distribution curve when the *F*-value is 0.474 and the degrees of freedom are 1 and 18?

What is the tail-end value when the *F*-value is 23.7 and the degrees of freedom are 3 and 6?

F–DISTRIBUTION

(TO END PROGRAM ENTER O)
F–VALUE? 0.474
DEGREES OF FREEDOM IN NUMERATOR? 1
DEGREES OF FREEDOM IN DENOMINATOR? 18
TAIL END VALUE = 0.5063

F–VALUE? 23.7
DEGREES OF FREEDOM IN NUMERATOR? 3
DEGREES OF FREEDOM IN DENOMINATOR? 6
TAIL END VALUE = 1.6E-03

F–VALUE? O

```
1 REM - OPTION 310
5 GRAPHICS O
10 PRINT "F-DISTRIBUTION"
   .
   .
   .
300 X=1-X
310 PRINT "TAIL END VALUE = ";X
320 PRINT
329 REM - RESTART PROGRAM
330 GOTO 40
340 END
```

Linear Correlation Coefficient

This program computes the coefficient of correlation between two variables. A linear relationship is assumed between the variables. You must enter the coordinates of a group of data points forming the regression line.

Example:

The height of twelve men and their sons is recorded in the table below. What is the coefficient of correlation between the heights of fathers and the heights of their sons?

Father	65	63	67	64	68	62	70	66	68	67	69	71
Son	68	66	68	65	69	66	68	65	71	67	68	70

Height in Inches

```
LINEAR CORRELATION COEFFICIENT

NUMBER OF POINTS? 12
X,Y OF POINT 1? 65,68
X,Y OF POINT 2? 63,66
X,Y OF POINT 3? 67,68
X,Y OF POINT 4? 64,65
X,Y OF POINT 5? 68,69
X,Y OF POINT 6? 62,66
X,Y OF POINT 7? 70,68
X,Y OF POINT 8? 66,65
X,Y OF POINT 9? 68,71
X,Y OF POINT 10? 67,67
X,Y OF POINT 11? 69,68
X,Y OF POINT 12? 71,70

CORRELATION COEFFICIENT = 0.7027844323

5 GRAPHICS O
10 PRINT "LINEAR CORRELATION COEFFICIENT"
20 PRINT
30 PRINT "NUMBER OF POINTS";
40 INPUT N
99 REM - ENTER COORDINATES OF DATA POINTS
100 FOR I=1 TO N
110 PRINT "X,Y OF POINT ";I;
120 INPUT X,Y
129 REM - ACCUMULATE INTERMEDIATE VALUES
130 J=J+X
140 K=K+Y
150 L=L+X^2
160 M=M+Y^2
170 R=R+X*Y
180 NEXT I
```

```
189 REM - CALCULATE COEFFICIENT, PRINT
190 R2=(N*R-J*K)/SQR((N*L-J^2)*(N*M-K^2))
200 PRINT
210 PRINT "CORRELATION COEFFICIENT = ";
215 PRINT R2
220 END
```

Linear Regression

This program fits a straight line to a given set of coordinates using the method of least squares. The equation of the line, coefficient of determination, coefficient of correlation, and standard error of estimate are printed. Once the line has been fitted, you may predict values of y for given values of x.

Example:

The table below shows the height and weight of 11 male college students. Fit a curve to these points. How much would the average 70 inches and 72 inches male student weigh?

Height (inches)	71	73	64	65	61	70	65	72	63	67	64
Weight (pounds)	160	183	154	168	159	180	145	210	132	168	141

```
LINEAR REGRESSION

NUMBER OF KNOWN POINTS? 11
X,Y OF POINT 1? 71,160
X,Y OF POINT 2? 73,183
X,Y OF POINT 3? 64,154
X,Y OF POINT 4? 65,168
X,Y OF POINT 5? 61,159
X,Y OF POINT 6? 70,180
X,Y OF POINT 7? 65,145
X,Y OF POINT 8? 72,210
X,Y OF POINT 9? 63,132
X,Y OF POINT 10? 67,168
X,Y OF POINT 11? 64,141

F(X) = -106.808628 + (4.04747608 * X)

COEFFICIENT OF DETERMINATION (R^2):
0.5562451056

COEFFICIENT OF CORRELATION:
0.7458184133

STANDARD ERROR OF ESTIMATE:
15.41444264

INTERPOLATION: (ENTER X=0 TO END)
X =? 70
Y = 176.514697

X =? 72
Y = 184.609649

X =? 0
```

```
5 GRAPHICS 0
10 PRINT "LINEAR REGRESSION"
20 PRINT
30 PRINT "NUMBER OF KNOWN POINTS";
40 INPUT N
99 REM - LOOP TO ENTER COORDINATES OF POINTS
100 FOR I=1 TO N
110 PRINT "X,Y OF POINT ";I;
120 INPUT X,Y
129 REM - ACCUMULATE INTERMEDIATE SUMS
130 J=J+X
140 K=K+Y
150 L=L+X^2
160 M=M+Y^2
170 R2=R2+X*Y
180 NEXT I
189 REM - COMPUTE CURVE COEFFICIENT
190 B=(N*R2-K*J)/(N*L-J^2)
200 A=(K-B*J)/N
210 PRINT
220 PRINT "F(X) = ";A;" + (";B;" * X)"
229 REM - COMPUTE REGRESSION ANAYLYSIS
230 J=B*(R2-J*K/N)
240 M=M-K^2/N
250 K=M-J
260 PRINT
270 R2=J/M
280 PRINT "COEFFICIENT OF DETERMINATION (R^2):"
282 PRINT R2
283 PRINT
290 PRINT "COEFFICIENT OF CORRELATION:"
291 PRINT SQR(R2)
292 PRINT
300 PRINT "STANDARD ERROR OF ESTIMATE:"
301 PRINT SQR(K/(N-2))
310 PRINT
319 REM - ESTIMATE Y-COORDINATES OF POINTS WITH ENTERED X-COORDINATES
320 PRINT "INTERPOLATION: ";
321 PRINT "(ENTER X=0 TO END)"
330 PRINT "X =";
340 INPUT X
349 REM - RESTART OR END PROGRAM? USER INPUT REQUIRED
350 IF X=0 THEN 390
360 PRINT "Y = ";A+B*X
370 PRINT
380 GOTO 330
390 END
```

Multiple Linear Regression

This program finds the coefficients of a multiple variable linear equation using the method of least squares. The equation is of the following form:

$$y = c + a_1x_1 + a_2x_2 + \dots a_nx_n$$

where: y = dependent variable
c = constant
$a_1, a_2, \dots, a_n$ = coefficients of independent variables $x_1, x_2, \dots, x_n$

The constant and the coefficients are printed.

   You must provide the x and y coordinates of known data points. Once the equation has been found using the data you enter, you may predict values of the dependent variables for given values of the independent variables.

   The dimension statement at line 30 limits the number of known data points the equation may contain. You can change this limit according to the following scheme:

30 DIM X($N+1$),S($N+1$),T($N+1$),A($N+1$,$N+2$)

where N = the number of known data points.

Example:

The table below shows the age, height, and weight of eight boys. Using weight as the dependent variable, fit a curve to the data. Estimate the weight of a seven-year old boy who is 51 inches tall.

Age	8	9	6	10	8	9	9	7
Height	48	49	44	59	55	51	55	50
Weight	59	55	50	80	61	75	67	58

```
MULTIPLE LINEAR REGRESSION

NUMBER OF KNOWN POINTS? 8
# OF INDEPENDENT VARIABLES? 2
POINT 1
 VARIABLE 1? 8
 VARIABLE 2? 48
 DEPENDENT VARIABLE? 59
POINT 2
 VARIABLE 1? 9
 VARIABLE 2? 49
 DEPENDENT VARIABLE? 55
POINT 3
 VARIABLE 1? 6
 VARIABLE 2? 44
 DEPENDENT VARIABLE? 50
POINT 4
 VARIABLE 1? 10
 VARIABLE 2? 59
```

```
 DEPENDENT VARIABLE? 80
POINT 5
 VARIABLE 1? 8
 VARIABLE 2? 55
 DEPENDENT VARIABLE? 61
POINT 6
 VARIABLE 1? 9
 VARIABLE 2? 51
 DEPENDENT VARIABLE? 75
POINT 7
 VARIABLE 1? 9
 VARIABLE 2? 55
 DEPENDENT VARIABLE? 67
POINT 8
 VARIABLE 1? 7
 VARIABLE 2? 50
 DEPENDENT VARIABLE? 58

EQUATION COEFFICIENTS:
      CONSTANT: -15.70212763
VARIABLE (1): 3.68085107
VARIABLE (2): 0.9432624108
COEFFICIENT OF DETERMINATION (R^2):
0.7157091735
COEFFICIENT OF MULTIPLE CORRELATION:
0.8459959654
STANDARD ERROR OF ESTIMATE:
6.42869322

INTERPOLATION:(ENTER 0 TO END PROGRAM)
VARIABLE 1? 7
VARIABLE 2? 51
DEPENDENT VARIABLE = 58.17021281

VARIABLE 1? 0
```

```
5 GRAPHICS 0
10 PRINT "MULTIPLE LINEAR REGRESSION"
20 PRINT
29 REM - SET ARRAY LIMITS TO X(N+1), S(N+1), T(N+1), A(N+1,N+2)
30 DIM X(9),S(9),T(9),A(9,10)
40 PRINT "NUMBER OF KNOWN POINTS";
50 INPUT N
60 PRINT "# OF INDEPENDENT VARIABLES";
70 INPUT V
80 X(1)=1
90 FOR I=1 TO N
100 PRINT "POINT ";I
110 FOR J=1 TO V
119 REM - ENTER INDEPENDENT VARIABLES FOR EACH POINT
120 PRINT " VARIABLE ";J;
130 INPUT X1
132 X(J+1)=X1
140 NEXT J
149 REM - ENTER DEPENDENT VARIABLE FOR EACH POINT
```

```
150 PRINT " DEPENDENT VARIABLE";
160 INPUT X1
162 X(V+2)=X1
169 REM - POPULATE A MATRIX TO BE USED IN CURVE FITTING
170 FOR K=1 TO V+1
180 FOR L=1 TO V+2
190 A(K,L)=A(K,L)+X(K)*X(L)
200 S(K)=A(K,V+2)
210 NEXT L
220 NEXT K
230 S(V+2)=S(V+2)+X(V+2)^2
240 NEXT I
248 REM - STATEMENTS 250 TO 500 FIT CURVE BY SOLVING THE SYSTEM OF;
249 REM - LINEAR EQUATIONS IN MATRIX A()
250 FOR I=2 TO V+1
260 T(I)=A(1,I)
270 NEXT I
280 FOR I=1 TO V+1
290 J=I
300 IF A(J,I)<>0 THEN 340
305 J=J+1
310 IF J<=V+1 THEN 300
320 PRINT "NO UNIQUE SOLUTION"
330 GOTO 810
340 FOR K=1 TO V+2
350 B=A(I,K)
360 A(I,K)=A(J,K)
370 A(J,K)=B
380 NEXT K
390 Z=1/A(I,I)
400 FOR K=1 TO V+2
410 A(I,K)=Z*A(I,K)
420 NEXT K
430 FOR J=1 TO V+1
440 IF J=I THEN 490
450 Z=-A(J,I)
460 FOR K=1 TO V+2
470 A(J,K)=A(J,K)+Z*A(I,K)
480 NEXT K
490 NEXT J
500 NEXT I
510 PRINT
520 PRINT "EQUATION COEFFICIENTS:"
525 PRINT "     CONSTANT: ";A(1,V+2)
530 FOR I=2 TO V+1
540 PRINT "VARIABLE (";I-1;"): ";A(I,V+2)
550 NEXT I
560 P=0
570 FOR I=2 TO V+1
580 P=P+A(I,V+2)*(S(I)-T(I)*S(1)/N)
590 NEXT I
600 R=S(V+2)-S(1)^2/N
610 Z=R-P
620 L=N-V-1
630 I=P/V
```

```
640 PRINT
650 I=P/R
660 PRINT "COEFFICIENT OF DETERMINATION (R^2):"
662 PRINT I
670 PRINT "COEFFICIENT OF MULTIPLE CORRELATION:"
675 PRINT SQR(I)
680 PRINT "STANDARD ERROR OF ESTIMATE:"
681 PRINT SQR(ABS(Z/L))
690 PRINT
699 REM - ESTIMATE DEPENDENT VARIABLE FROM ENTERED INDEPENDENT VARABLES
700 PRINT "INTERPOLATION:";
701 PRINT "(ENTER 0 TO END PROGRAM)"
710 P=A(1,V+2)
720 FOR J=1 TO V
730 PRINT "VARIABLE ";J;
740 INPUT X
749 REM - TEST FOR END OF PROGRAM
750 IF X=0 THEN 810
760 P=P+A(J+1,V+2)*X
770 NEXT J
780 PRINT "DEPENDENT VARIABLE = ";P
790 PRINT
799 REM - RETURN FOR MORE DATA
800 GOTO 710
810 END
```

*N*th Order Regression

This program finds the coefficients of an *N*th order equation using the method of least squares. The equation is of the following form:

$$y = c + a_1x + a_2x^2 + \ldots a_nx^n$$

$$\text{where: } y = \text{dependent variable}$$
$$c = \text{constant}$$
$$a_1, a_2, \ldots, a_n = \text{coefficients of independent variables } x, x^2, \ldots, x^n, \text{ respectively}$$

The equation coefficients, coefficient of determination, coefficient of correlation, and standard error of estimate are printed.

You must provide the x and y coordinates for known data points. Once the equation has been computed you may predict values of y for given values of x.

The dimension statement at line 30 limits the degree of the equation. You can change this limit according to the following scheme:

$$\text{30 DIM A}(2 \cdot D+1), \text{R}(D+1, D+2), \text{T}(D+2)$$

where D = maximum degree of equation.

Example:

The table below gives the stopping distance (reaction plus braking distance) of an automobile at various speeds. Fit an exponential curve to the data. Estimate the stopping distance at 55 m.p.h.

M.P.H.	20	30	40	50	60	70
Stopping distance	54	90	138	206	292	396

```
N´TH ORDER REGRESSION

DEGREE OF EQUATION? 2
NUMBER OF KNOWN POINTS? 6
X,Y OF POINT 1? 20,54
X,Y OF POINT 2? 30,90
X,Y OF POINT 3? 40,138
X,Y OF POINT 4? 50,206
X,Y OF POINT 5? 60,292
X,Y OF POINT 6? 70,396

          CONSTANT = 41.753171
1 DEGREE COEFFICIENT = -1.09477737
2 DEGREE COEFFICIENT = 0.0878468501

COEFFICIENT OF DETERMINATION (R^2):
0.9999250511
CORRELATION COEFFICIENT:
0.9999625248
STANDARD ERROR OF ESTIMATE:
1.44933317
```

```
INTERPOLATION: (ENTER O TO END)
X =? 55
Y = 247.277127

X =? O


5 GRAPHICS O
10 PRINT "N^TH ORDER REGRESSION"
20 PRINT
28 REM - SET LIMITS OF DEGREE OF EQUATION TO A(2D+1), R(D+1),D+2), T(D+2)
29 REM - (WHERE D=MAXIMUM DEGREE OF EQUATION)
30 DIM A(13),R(7,8),T(8)
40 PRINT "DEGREE OF EQUATION";
50 INPUT D
52 FOR X=1 TO 2*D+1
53 A(X)=0
54 NEXT X
55 FOR X=1 TO D+2
56 T(X)=0
57 NEXT X
60 PRINT "NUMBER OF KNOWN POINTS";
70 INPUT N
80 A(1)=N
89 REM - ENTER COORDINATES OF DATA POINTS
90 FOR I=1 TO N
100 PRINT "X,Y OF POINT ";I;
110 INPUT X,Y
119 REM - LINES 120 TO 200 POPULATE MATRICES WITH A SYSTEM OF EQUATIONS
120 FOR J=2 TO 2*D+1
130 A(J)=A(J)+X^(J-1)
140 NEXT J
150 FOR K=1 TO D+1
160 R(K,D+2)=T(K)+Y*X^(K-1)
170 T(K)=T(K)+Y*X^(K-1)
180 NEXT K
190 T(D+2)=T(D+2)+Y^2
200 NEXT I
209 REM - LINES 210 TO 490 SOLVE THE SYSTEM OF EQUATIONS IN THE MATRICES
210 FOR J=1 TO D+1
220 FOR K=1 TO D+1
230 R(J,K)=A(J+K-1)
240 NEXT K
250 NEXT J
260 FOR J=1 TO D+1
270 FOR K=J TO D+1
280 IF R(K,J)<>0 THEN 320
290 NEXT K
300 PRINT "NO UNIQUE SOLUTION"
310 GOTO 790
320 FOR I=1 TO D+2
330 S=R(J,I)
340 R(J,I)=R(K,I)
350 R(K,I)=S
360 NEXT I
370 Z=1/R(J,J)
```

```
380 FOR I=1 TO D+2
390 R(J,I)=Z*R(J,I)
400 NEXT I
410 FOR K=1 TO D+1
420 IF K=J THEN 470
430 Z=-R(K,J)
440 FOR I=1 TO D+2
450 R(K,I)=R(K,I)+Z*R(J,I)
460 NEXT I
470 NEXT K
480 NEXT J
490 PRINT
495 PRINT "                 CONSTANT = ";
496 PRINT R(1,D+2)
499 REM - PRINT EQUATION COEFFICIENTS
500 FOR J=1 TO D
510 PRINT J;" DEGREE COEFFICIENT = ";
511 PRINT R(J+1,D+2)
520 NEXT J
530 PRINT
539 REM - COMPUTE REGRESSION ANALYSIS
540 P=0
550 FOR J=2 TO D+1
560 P=P+R(J,D+2)*(T(J)-A(J)*T(1)/N)
570 NEXT J
580 Q=T(D+2)-T(1)^2/N
590 Z=Q-P
600 I=N-D-1
620 PRINT
630 J=P/Q
640 PRINT "COEFFICIENT OF DETERMINATION (R^2):"
642 PRINT J
650 PRINT "CORRELATION COEFFICIENT:"
651 PRINT SQR(J)
660 PRINT "STANDARD ERROR OF ESTIMATE:"
661 PRINT SQR(Z/I)
670 PRINT
679 REM - COMPUTE Y-COORDINATE FROM ENTERED X-COORDINATE
680 PRINT "INTERPOLATION: ";
681 PRINT "(ENTER 0 TO END)"
690 P=R(1,D+2)
700 PRINT "X =";
710 INPUT X
720 IF X=0 THEN 790
730 FOR J=1 TO D
740 P=P+R(J+1,D+2)*X^J
750 NEXT J
760 PRINT "Y = ";P
770 PRINT
780 GOTO 690
790 END
```

Geometric Regression

This program fits a geometric curve to a set of coordinates using the method of least squares. The equation, coefficient of determination, coefficient of correlation, and standard error of estimate are printed.

You must provide the x and y coordinates of known data points. Once the curve has been fitted you may predict values of y for given values of x.

Example:

The table below give the pressures of a gas measured at various volumes in an experiment. The relationship between pressure and volume of a gas is expressed by the following formula:

$$PV^K = C$$

where: P = pressure
V = volume
C and K are constants

This formula can be rewritten in standard geometric form:

$$P = CV^{-K}$$

Note the exponent is negative, which accounts for the negative exponents the program calculates.

Fit a geometric curve to the data and estimate the pressure of 90 cubic inches of the gas.

Volume	56.1	60.7	73.2	88.3	120.1	187.5
Pressure	57.0	51.0	39.2	30.2	19.6	10.5

```
GEOMETRIC REGRESSION

NUMBER OF KNOWN POINTS? 6
X,Y OF POINT 1? 56.1,57
X,Y OF POINT 2? 60.7,51
X,Y OF POINT 3? 73.2,39.2
X,Y OF POINT 4? 88.3,30.2
X,Y OF POINT 5? 120.1,19.6
X,Y OF POINT 6? 187.5,10.5

F(X) = 16103.5638 * X^-1.40154885

COEFFICIENT OF DETERMINATION (R^2):
0.9999860276

COEFFICIENT OF CORRELATION:
0.9999930137

STANDARD ERROR OF ESTIMATE:
2.674883175E-03

INTERPOLATION:(X=0 TO END)
X =? 90
```

```
Y = 29.3734994

X =? 0


5 GRAPHICS 0
10 PRINT "GEOMETRIC REGRESSION"
20 PRINT
30 PRINT "NUMBER OF KNOWN POINTS";
40 INPUT N
99 REM - ENTER COORDINATES OF DATA POINTS
100 FOR I=1 TO N
110 PRINT "X,Y OF POINT ";I;
120 INPUT X,Y
129 REM - ACCUMULATE INTERMEDIATE VALUES
130 Y=LOG(Y)
140 X=LOG(X)
150 J=J+X
160 K=K+Y
170 L=L+X^2
180 M=M+Y^2
190 R2=R2+X*Y
200 NEXT I
209 REM - CALCULATE AND PRINT COEFFICIENTS OF EQUATION
210 B=(N*R2-K*J)/(N*L-J^2)
220 A=(K-B*J)/N
230 PRINT
240 PRINT "F(X) = ";EXP(A);" * X^";B
249 REM - CALCULATE REGRESSION ANALYSIS
250 J=B*(R2-J*K/N)
260 M=M-K^2/N
270 K=M-J
280 PRINT
290 R2=J/M
300 PRINT "COEFFICIENT OF DETERMINATION (R^2):"
305 PRINT R2
306 PRINT
310 PRINT "COEFFICIENT OF CORRELATION:"
311 PRINT SQR(R2)
315 PRINT
320 PRINT "STANDARD ERROR OF ESTIMATE:"
325 PRINT SQR(K/(N-2))
326 PRINT
330 PRINT
339 REM - ESTIMATE Y-COORDINATE FROM ENTERED X-COORDINATE
340 PRINT "INTERPOLATION:";
341 PRINT "(X=0 TO END)"
350 PRINT "X =";
360 INPUT X
369 REM - RESTART OR END PROGRAM? USER INPUT REQUIRED
370 IF X=0 THEN 410
380 PRINT "Y = ";EXP(A)*X^B
390 PRINT
399 REM - RETURN FOR MORE DATA
400 GOTO 350
410 END
```

Exponential Regression

This program finds the coefficients of an equation for an exponential curve. The equation is in the following form:

$$f(x) = ae^{bx}$$

where a and b are the calculated coefficients

The equation coefficients, coefficient of determination, coefficient of correlation, and standard error of estimate are printed.

You must provide the x and y coordinates for known data points. Once the curve has been fitted you may predict values of y for given values of x.

Example:

The table below shows the number of bacteria present in a culture at various points in time. Fit an exponential curve to the data and estimate the number of bacteria after seven hours.

Number of Hours	0	1	2	3	4	5	6
Number of Bacteria	25	38	58	89	135	206	315

```
EXPONENTIAL REGRESSION

NUMBER OF KNOWN POINTS? 7
X,Y OF POINT 1? 0,25
X,Y OF POINT 2? 1,38
X,Y OF POINT 3? 2,58
X,Y OF POINT 4? 3,89
X,Y OF POINT 5? 4,135
X,Y OF POINT 6? 5,206
X,Y OF POINT 7? 6,315


A = 24.9616401
B = 0.4223753793

COEFFICIENT OF DETERMINATION (R^2):
1.00000505

COEFFICIENT OF CORRELATION:
1.00000252

STANDARD ERROR OF ESTIMATE:
2.247665456E-03

INTERPOLATION:
(X=0 TO END)
X =? 7
Y =480.087256

X =? 0
```

```
5 GRAPHICS O
10 PRINT "EXPONENTIAL REGRESSION"
20 PRINT
30 PRINT "NUMBER OF KNOWN POINTS";
40 INPUT N
50 J=0
60 K=0
70 L=0
80 M=0
90 R2=0
99 REM - ENTER COORDINATES OF DATA POINTS
100 FOR I=1 TO N
110 PRINT "X,Y OF POINT ";I;
120 INPUT X,Y
129 REM - ACCUMULATE INTERMEDIATE VALUES
130 Y=LOG(Y)
140 J=J+X
150 K=K+Y
160 L=L+X^2
170 M=M+Y^2
180 R2=R2+X*Y
190 NEXT I
199 REM - CALCULATE AND PRINT COEFFICIENTS OF EQUATION
200 B=(N*R2-K*J)/(N*L-J^2)
210 A=(K-B*J)/N
220 PRINT
230 PRINT "A = ";EXP(A)
240 PRINT "B = ";B
249 REM - CALCULATE REGRESSION TABLE VALUES
250 J=B*(R2-J*K/N)
260 M=M-K^2/N
270 K=M-J
280 PRINT
290 R2=J/M
300 PRINT "COEFFICIENT OF DETERMINATION (R^2):"
302 PRINT R2
306 PRINT
310 PRINT "COEFFICIENT OF CORRELATION:"
312 PRINT SQR(R2)
316 PRINT
320 PRINT "STANDARD ERROR OF ESTIMATE:"
322 PRINT SQR(ABS(K/(N-2)))
326 PRINT
330 PRINT
339 REM - ESTIMATE Y-VALUE FROM ENTERED X-VALUE
340 PRINT "INTERPOLATION:"
341 PRINT "(X=0 TO END)"
350 PRINT "X =";
360 INPUT X
370 IF X=0 THEN 410
380 PRINT "Y =";EXP(A)*EXP(B*X)
390 PRINT
399 REM - RETURN FOR MORE DATA
400 GOTO 350
410 END
```

System Reliability

This program calculates the reliability of an operating system that is subject to wearout and chance failure. You must enter the system's operating time and the wearout time and failure rate of each component.

Example:

Compute the reliability of a computer system operating for 1000 hours with the components shown in the list below.

	Wearout (hours)	Failure
CPU	15,000	0.00020
Terminal	3,000	0.00010
Disk	3,000	0.00015
Printer	1,500	0.00015

```
SYSTEM RELIABILITY

(TO END PROGRAM ENTER 0)
OPERATING TIME IN HOURS? 1000
NUMBER OF COMPONENTS? 4

COMPONENT 1
AVERAGE WEAROUT TIME? 15000
AVERAGE FAILURE RATE? 2E-04

COMPONENT 2
AVERAGE WEAROUT TIME? 3000
AVERAGE FAILURE RATE? 1E-04

COMPONENT 3
AVERAGE WEAROUT TIME? 3000
AVERAGE FAILURE RATE? 1.5E-04

COMPONENT 4
AVERAGE WEAROUT TIME? 1500
AVERAGE FAILURE RATE? 1.5E-04

SYSTEM RELIABILITY = 0.1353352872

OPERATING TIME IN HOURS? 0

5 GRAPHICS 0
10 PRINT "SYSTEM RELIABILITY"
20 PRINT
30 PRINT "(TO END PROGRAM ENTER 0)"
40 PRINT "OPERATING TIME IN HOURS";
50 INPUT T
```

```
59 REM - TEST FOR END OF PROGRAM
60 IF T=0 THEN 230
70 PRINT "NUMBER OF COMPONENTS";
80 INPUT N
90 Z=0
99 REM - ENTER DATA FOR EACH COMPONENT
100 FOR I=1 TO N
105 PRINT
110 PRINT "COMPONENT ";I
120 PRINT "AVERAGE WEAROUT TIME";
130 INPUT W
140 PRINT "AVERAGE FAILURE RATE";
150 INPUT F
159 REM - INCLUDE EACH COMPONENT IN RELIABILITY
160 Z=Z+1/W+F
170 NEXT I
180 PRINT
189 REM - CALCULATE RELIABILITY, PRINT
190 Z=EXP(-Z*T)
200 PRINT "SYSTEM RELIABILITY = ";Z
210 PRINT
219 REM - RESTART PROGRAM
220 GOTO 40
230 END
```

Average Growth Rate, Future Projections

This program calculates the average growth rate of a company, then projects figures for future years. The growth rate and projections could be computed for any aspect of a company, such as sales, earnings, number of employees, or patronage. You must provide established figures for a past series of years.

The dimension statement at line 30 limits the number of past figures you may enter. Any alteration of this limit should be done in the following manner:

$$30 \ \text{DIM} \ S(N)$$

where N = the number of years for which figures are known.

Example:

The borrowing records for Claremount County Library are tabulated in the graph below. What is its average growth rate? How many books can it expect to lend in its tenth and twentieth years of service?

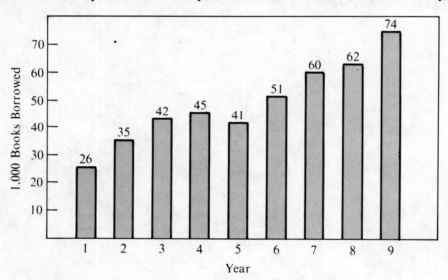

```
AVERAGE GROWTH RATE,
FUTURE PROJECTIONS

NUMBER OF YEARS FIGURES ESTABLISHED? 9
FIGURE: YEAR 1? 26
        YEAR 2? 35
        YEAR 3? 42
        YEAR 4? 45
        YEAR 5? 41
        YEAR 6? 51
        YEAR 7? 60
        YEAR 8? 62
        YEAR 9? 74
AVERAGE GROWTH RATE = 11.88%
```

```
(ENTER 0 TO END PROGRAM)
PROJECTED SALES FOR YEAR? 10
                     = 81.29
PROJECTED SALES FOR YEAR? 20
                     = 249.87
PROJECTED SALES FOR YEAR? 0


5 GRAPHICS 0
10 PRINT "AVERAGE GROWTH RATE,"
15 PRINT "FUTURE PROJECTIONS"
20 PRINT
29 REM - SET ARRAY S TO THE NUMBER OF YEARS FOR WHICH FIGURES ARE KNOWN
30 DIM S(20)
40 PRINT "NUMBER OF YEARS FIGURES ESTABLISHED";
50 INPUT N
60 FOR I=1 TO N
70 IF I>1 THEN 100
80 PRINT "FIGURE: YEAR ";I;
90 GOTO 110
100 PRINT "          YEAR ";I;
110 INPUT X
112 S(I)=X
120 NEXT I
129 REM - INITIALIZE VARIABLES FOR FIRST YEAR
130 T=LOG(S(1))
140 V=0
149 REM - LOOP FOR REMAINING YEARS OF HISTORY
150 FOR I=2 TO N
160 L=LOG(S(I))
170 T=T+L
180 V=V+(I-1)*L
190 NEXT I
199 REM - CALCULATE AVERAGE GROWTH RATE
200 A=6*(2*V/(N-1)-T)/(N)/(N+1)
210 G=EXP(A)-1
219 REM - ROUND OFF, PRINT
220 PRINT "AVERAGE GROWTH RATE = ";
225 PRINT INT(G*10000+0.5)/100;"%"
230 PRINT
239 REM - CALCULATE AVERAGE ANNUAL GROWTH FACTOR
240 S=EXP(T/N-A*(N-1)/2)
250 PRINT "(ENTER 0 TO END PROGRAM)"
259 REM - INPUT YEAR NUMBER
260 PRINT "PROJECTED SALES FOR YEAR";
270 INPUT Y1
279 REM - TEST FOR END OF PROGRAM
280 IF Y1=0 THEN 320
289 REM - CALCULATE  PROJECTED SALES FIGURE
290 S1=S*(1+G)^(Y1-1)
299 REM - ROUND OFF, PRINT
300 PRINT "                     = ";
305 PRINT INT(S1*100+0.5)/100
309 REM - RETURN FOR MORE DATA
310 GOTO 260
320 END
```

Federal Withholding Taxes

This program calculates the amount of federal income and FICA taxes withheld from one's earnings. You must provide employee information regarding marital status, the number of exemptions claimed, the amount of taxable pay, and year-to-date taxable pay.

The number of pay periods per year is established at line 80. If your pay period is other than monthly, you must alter this statement to set *N* equal to the number of pay periods per year.

There is a considerable amount of tax information which may change from year to year. The values listed in the data tables at lines 30 and 40 are among those that may need periodic revision. The annual values for single and married persons should be compared each year with those listed in Table 7 of the current IRS Circular E.

The annual FICA rate, the FICA cutoff amount, and the annual amount of withholding allowance may also need revision. The values established at lines 50, 60, and 70 should also be compared to those listed in the current IRS circular.

Annual rates and cutoffs are used irrespective of your actual pay period frequency. The program automatically adjusts them to match your pay period.

Examples:

Judy earns $900.00 per month. The payroll clerk is figuring her March paycheck. Judy is single and claims only herself as as a dependent. What amounts are withheld from her paycheck?

Dr. Berger has earned $2600.00 this month. So far this year she has grossed $26,000.00. She is married and claims four dependents. What amounts will be withheld this month for the federal government?

```
FEDERAL WITHHOLDING TAXES

MARITAL STATUS (1=SINGLE,2=MARRIED)? 1
WITHHOLDING TAX EXEMPTIONS? 1
TAXABLE PAY? 900
YTD TAXABLE PAY? 1800
TAXABLE = $900
INCOME TAX = $128.5
FICA = $55.17
MORE DATA (1=YES, 0=NO)? 1


MARITAL STATUS (1=SINGLE,2=MARRIED)? 2
WITHHOLDING TAX EXEMPTIONS? 4
TAXABLE PAY? 2600
YTD TAXABLE PAY? 26000
TAXABLE = $2600
INCOME TAX = $471.42
FICA = $0
MORE DATA (1=YES, 0=NO)? 0


5 GRAPHICS 0
10 PRINT "FEDERAL WITHHOLDING TAXES"
20 PRINT
25 REM - THE FOLLOWING DATA CONTAINS
```

```
60 PRINT "INGREDIENT ";I;":"
70 PRINT "STORE COST FOR BULK UNIT";
80 INPUT C
90 PRINT "NUMBER OF UNITS IN BULK";
100 INPUT U
110 PRINT "RECIPE UNITS PER ";
111 PRINT "BULK UNIT";
120 INPUT F
130 PRINT "NUMBER OF RECIPE ";
131 PRINT "UNITS NEEDED";
140 INPUT R
149 REM - SUM COST OF EACH INGREDIENT PER AMOUNT USED
150 P=P+C/U/F*R
160 NEXT I
165 PRINT
170 PRINT "NUMBER OF SERVINGS";
180 INPUT S
190 PRINT
199 REM - ROUND OFF COSTS TO NEAREST CENT, PRINT RESULTS
200 PRINT "TOTAL COST FOR ";
201 PRINT "ONE RECIPE = $";
205 PRINT INT(P*100+0.5)/100
210 PRINT "COST PER SERVING = $";
215 PRINT INT(P/S*100+0.5)/100
220 PRINT
229 REM - CALCULATE ALTERNATIVE PRICE PER SERVING
230 PRINT "CHANGE NUMBER OF SERVINGS"
231 PRINT "(1=YES, 0=NO)";
240 INPUT N
250 IF N=1 THEN 170
260 END
```

OPTION

As you become familiar with the operation of this program you may wish to shorten it by entering the information required for each ingredient on one line. The necessary program changes are listed following the example below.

Example:

Calculate the cost per serving of strawberry shortcake in the previous example when it is served without cream.

```
RECIPE COST

NUMBER OF INGREDIENTS? 8

INGREDIENT 1:
? 1.59,5,2.5,3
```

Survey Check (Map Check)

Courtesy: Robert Irving
Northridge,
California

This program calculates the error of closure and area of a plot for which a traverse of the perimeter is available. The program will also calculate how far North and East the end of an open traverse is from its origin (the Northing and Easting). The local coordinates of the origin can be entered for an open traverse. Negative values of Northing and Easting are South and West, respectively, of the 0,0 origin of the survey.

The individual legs of the traverse may be either straight lines or arcs of circles. To compute the traverse, you must have the bearing and length of each straight leg. You also need the radius, bearing of chord, and length of chord (or radius, arc measure, and bearing of a tangent) for each curved leg.

For a closed survey, pick any intersection of legs as a starting point, and number the lines and arcs, starting with one, in a *clockwise* direction around the perimeter. If any arc is 180 degrees or more, it must be broken into smaller arcs, each less than 180 degrees.

By convention, surveyors measure bearings East and West of North and South, as shown in the following figure. This convention was established in the days before computers, so that trigonometric functions could be easily looked up in tables not exceeding 90 degrees. For each leg, you must enter the quadrant number and the degrees, minutes, and seconds East or West of the North-South axis. The program will indicate the direction of the leg (e.g., SW), and will convert the quadrant, degrees, etc. to an azimuth angle. Azimuth is measured clockwise from North to 360 degrees.

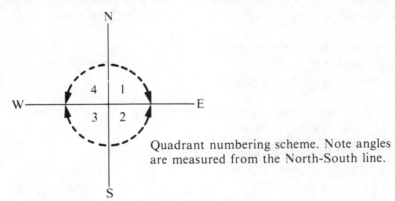

Quadrant numbering scheme. Note angles are measured from the North-South line.

A curved leg, or arc, is defined by two auxiliary legs, each of which is a radius of the arc. The bearing of the first auxiliary leg is the direction of the radius from the first encountered end of the arc to the center of the arc. You can compute this bearing from the bearing of the arc's tangent at that point, since the radius is perpendicular to the tangent. The survey may show the bearing of the tangent. If not, you can compute it by adding one half the angular extent of the arc to the bearing of the arc's chord, as shown in the next figure.

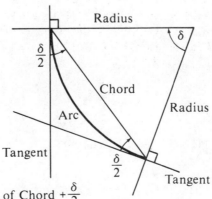

Bearing of Tangent = Bearing of Chord $+ \dfrac{\delta}{2}$

The bearing of the second radius is from the center of the arc to the other end, and the distance is entered as a *negative* number to signal to the computer that this and the prior leg are not perimeter legs, but auxiliary legs of an arc.

The program asks you for the bearing and distance of each leg by number. Legs are entered in sets of ten (or less). Following the last entry in a set, you can correct any leg in the set. You must enter both auxiliary legs of an arc in the same set. You can enter a bearing of zero to end one set, and then enter more legs on the next set.

When you have corrected a set, a traverse table is printed for the set. This includes each leg number, direction, azimuth angle, and distance, and incremental and cumulative Northing and Easting. The cumulative Northing and Easting after the last leg on a closed survey gives the error of closure. Arc angle, radius, sector area, chord length, and tangent length are printed between the two auxiliary legs of each curved leg.

Following the printout of the last leg of a closed survey, the area of the plot will be printed, both in square feet and in acres. The area computed is very accurate provided two conditions are met:

1. The error of closure is small (0.01 feet is usual for a house lot), and

2. The area is sufficiently small that curvature of the earth does not become significant. Surveys covering several tens of miles have to account for this latter factor.

Example:

The figure below illustrates the boundaries of a lot with one curved side. The leg numbers are circled. Bearings and distances are shown for each leg. Find the error of closure and lot area.

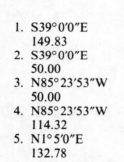
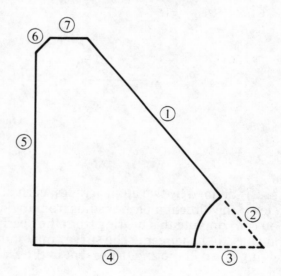

1. S39°0'0"E
   149.83
2. S39°0'0"E
   50.00
3. N85°23'53"W
   50.00
4. N85°23'53"W
   114.32
5. N1°5'0"E
   132.78
6. N46°0'0"E
   14.00
7. S89°0'0"E
   25.46

```
MAP CHECK

OPEN (1) OR CLOSED (0) SURVEY? 0

NEXT SET OF  LEGS:

LEG NO. 1
QUADRANT,DEGREES, MINUTES,SECONDS
? 2,39,0,0
DISTANCE
(NEGATIVE IF OUTWARD RADIUS)? 149.83
```

```
LEG NO. 2
QUADRANT,DEGREES, MINUTES,SECONDS
? 2,39,0,0
DISTANCE
(NEGATIVE IF OUTWARD RADIUS)? 50

LEG NO. 3
QUADRANT,DEGREES, MINUTES,SECONDS
? 4,85,23,53
DISTANCE
(NEGATIVE IF OUTWARD RADIUS)? -50

LEG NO. 4
QUADRANT,DEGREES, MINUTES,SECONDS
? 4,85,23,53
DISTANCE
(NEGATIVE IF OUTWARD RADIUS)? 114.32

LEG NO. 5
QUADRANT,DEGREES, MINUTES,SECONDS
? 1,1,5,0
DISTANCE
(NEGATIVE IF OUTWARD RADIUS)? 132.78

LEG NO. 6
QUADRANT,DEGREES, MINUTES,SECONDS
? 1,46,0,0
DISTANCE
(NEGATIVE IF OUTWARD RADIUS)? 14

LEG NO. 7
QUADRANT,DEGREES, MINUTES,SECONDS
? 2,89,0,0
DISTANCE
(NEGATIVE IF OUTWARD RADIUS)? 25.46

LEG NO. 8
QUADRANT,DEGREES, MINUTES,SECONDS
? 0,0,0,0
CORRECT WHICH LEG IN THIS SET
        (0=NO MORE CHANGES)? 0
ORIGIN 0 / 0

LEG/DIR.         1 / SE
AZIMUTH/DIST.    = 141 0 0 / 149.83
DEL N/DEL E      = -116.43968 / 94.29119616
NORTHING/EASTING = -116.43968 / 94.29119616

LEG/DIR.         2 / SE
AZIMUTH/DIST.    = 141 0 0 / 50
DEL N/DEL E      = -38.85726511 / 31.46606025
NORTHING/EASTING = -155.296945 / 125.757256

PRESS 'RETURN' FOR NEXT SET OF LEGS?
```

```
 ARC:   46 23 53
R= 50   A= 2024.497063   C= 39.39263084   T= 54.3985565


LEG/DIR.          3 / NW
AZIMUTH/DIST.     = 274 36 7 / 50
DEL N/DEL E       = 4.01158153 / -49.83881252
NORTHING/EASTING = -151.285364 / 75.918444


LEG/DIR.          4 / NW
AZIMUTH/DIST.     = 274 36 7 / 114.32
DEL N/DEL E       = 9.17208002 / -113.95146
NORTHING/EASTING = -142.113284 / -38.033016


PRESS 'RETURN' FOR NEXT SET OF LEGS?


LEG/DIR.          5 / NE
AZIMUTH/DIST.     = 1 4 60 / 132.78
DEL N/DEL E       = 132.756265 / 2.51041923
NORTHING/EASTING = -9.357019 / -35.52259677


LEG/DIR.          6 / NE
AZIMUTH/DIST.     = 46 0 0 / 14
DEL N/DEL E       = 9.72521719 / 10.07075725
NORTHING/EASTING = 0.36819819 / -25.45183952


PRESS 'RETURN' FOR NEXT SET OF LEGS?


LEG/DIR.          7 / SE
AZIMUTH/DIST.     = 91 0 0 / 25.46
DEL N/DEL E       = -0.4443338241 / 25.45612243
NORTHING/EASTING = -0.0761356341 / 4.28291E-03


ANY MORE LEGS (1=YES, 0=NO)? 0
PLOT AREA IS 13347.6721 SQ. FT.

PLOT AREA IS 0.30642039 ACRES

5 GRAPHICS 0
6 DIM W$(1)
10 REM - SURVEY CHECK
12 REM - FOR CLOSED SURVEY FOLLOW TRAVERSE CLOCKWISE
13 REM - KEEP PLOT TO RIGHT OF EACH PERIMETER LEG
14 REM - COMPUTE AUXILIARY LEGS AS RADII AT EACH
15 REM - END OF ARC.  ARC<180 DEGREES
16 REM
19 REM - KO = NUMBER OF LEGS PER SET
20 KO=10
30 DIM B(10),L(10)
49 REM - R IS THE CONVERSION FACTOR FOR DEGREES TO RADIANS
50 R=0.0174532925
52 REM - VALUE OF PI; PI=3.14159265
55 P1=3.14159265
60 PRINT "MAP CHECK":PRINT
70 PRINT "OPEN (1) OR CLOSED (0) SURVEY";
80 INPUT F
```

```
90 IF F=0 THEN 120
100 PRINT "ORIGIN: NORTHING, EASTING";
110 INPUT N,E
120 PRINT
122 PRINT "NEXT SET OF  LEGS:"
124 PRINT
125 G=H
130 FOR K=1 TO KO
139 REM - INPUT BEARING AND DISTANCE FOR NEXT LEG
140 GOSUB 2000
149 REM - IF BEARING IS 0, END INPUT FOR THIS SET
150 IF Q=0 THEN 170
155 G=G+1
160 GOTO 240
169 REM - ZERO UNUSED LEGS IN THIS SET
170 IF K=KO THEN 230
180 FOR J=K+1 TO KO
190 B(J)=0
200 L(J)=0
210 NEXT J
230 K=KO
240 NEXT K
260 PRINT "CORRECT WHICH LEG IN THIS SET"
261 PRINT "          (0=NO MORE CHANGES)";
270 INPUT K
279 REM - NO CHANGES IF 0 INPUT
280 IF K=0 THEN 310
285 K=K-H
290 GOSUB 2000
300 GOTO 260
309 REM - COMPUTE VALUES AND PRINT TRAVERSE TABLE
310 GRAPHICS 0
320 PRINT "ORIGIN ";N;" / ";E
340 PRINT
350 FOR K=1 TO KO
360 L1=L(K)
361 Z=Z+1
369 REM - CHECK FOR ARC
370 IF L1<0 THEN 1100
380 IF L1=0 THEN 900
388 REM - COMPUTE NORTHING/EASTING INCREMENT (CONVERT BEARINGS FROM
389 REM - DEGREES TO RADIANS)
390 L=L(K)*COS(B(K)*R)
400 D=L(K)*SIN(B(K)*R)
410 N=N+L
420 E=E+D
429 REM - INCREMENT AREA
430 A=A-E*L+N*D
440 PRINT "LEG/DIR.       ";H+K;" / ";
449 REM - FROM BEARING, DETERMINE DIRECTION
450 IF B(K)=0 THEN 470
460 GOTO 490
470 PRINT "N"
480 GOTO 830
490 IF B(K)<90 THEN 510
```

```
500 GOTO 530
510 PRINT "NE"
520 GOTO 830
530 IF B(K)=90 THEN 550
540 GOTO 570
550 PRINT "E"
560 GOTO 830
570 IF B(K)<180 THEN 590
580 GOTO 610
590 PRINT "SE"
600 GOTO 830
610 IF B(K)=180 THEN 630
620 GOTO 650
630 PRINT "S"
640 GOTO 830
650 IF B(K)<270 THEN 670
660 GOTO 690
670 PRINT "SW"
680 GOTO 830
690 IF B(K)=270 THEN 710
700 GOTO 730
710 PRINT "W"
720 GOTO 830
730 IF B(K)<360 THEN 750
740 GOTO 770
750 PRINT "NW"
760 GOTO 830
770 IF B(K)=360 THEN 790
780 GOTO 810
790 PRINT "N"
800 GOTO 830
810 B(K)=B(K)-360
820 GOTO 450
829 REM - BREAK BEARING INTO DEGREES, MINUTES, SECONDS
830 D1=INT(B(K))
840 M1=(B(K)-D1)*60
850 M=INT(M1)
860 S=INT((M1-M)*60+0.5)
870 PRINT "AZIMUTH/DIST.     = ";
872 PRINT D1;" ";M;" ";S;" / ";L(K)
880 PRINT "DEL N/DEL E       = ";
881 PRINT L;" / ";D
882 PRINT "NORTHING/EASTING = ";
883 PRINT N;" / ";E
885 PRINT
890 L(K)=L1
891 IF Z<2 THEN 900
895 PRINT "PRESS 'RETURN' FOR NEXT SET OF LEGS";
896 INPUT W$
897 PRINT
898 Z=0
900 NEXT K
910 H=G
920 PRINT "ANY MORE LEGS (1=YES, 0=NO)";
930 INPUT U
```

```
940 IF U<>0 THEN 120
949 REM - NO AREA FOR OPEN SURVEY
950 IF F<>0 THEN 1000
960 A=ABS(A/2)
970 PRINT "PLOT AREA IS ";A;" SQ. FT."
980 PRINT
990 PRINT "PLOT AREA IS ";INT(A/43560*100000000+0.5)/100000000;" ACRES"
1000 GOTO 2280
1099 REM - CALCULATE CURVED LEG AND PRINT ON TRANSVERSE TABLE
1100 C=ABS(B(K)-B(K-1))
1110 C=ABS(180-C)
1120 D=-L1
1130 L(K)=D
1140 A1=C/180*P1*D*D
1150 C1=2*D*SIN(C/2*R)
1160 T=D*(SGN(C/2*R)/COS(C/2*R))
1170 B9=B(K)-B(K-1)
1180 IF B9<-180 THEN 1210
1190 IF B9>180 THEN 1210
1200 IF B9>0 THEN 1230
1210 A=A+A1
1220 GOTO 1240
1230 A=A-A1
1240 D1=INT(C)
1250 M1=(C-D1)*60
1260 M=INT(M1)
1270 S=INT((M1-M)*60+0.5)
1280 PRINT " ARC:   ";
1281 PRINT D1;" ";M;" ";S
1282 PRINT "R= ";D;"   A= ";A1;
1290 PRINT "  C= ";C1;"   T= ";T
1300 PRINT
1320 GOTO 390
1999 REM - INPUT DATA FOR ONE LEG
2000 B(K)=0
2010 L(K)=0
2020 PRINT "LEG NO. ";H+K
2021 PRINT "QUADRANT,DEGREES, ";
2022 PRINT "MINUTES,SECONDS"
2030 INPUT Q,D,M,S
2040 IF Q=0 THEN 2270
2050 IF Q>4 THEN 2020
2060 IF Q<0 THEN 2020
2070 IF D<0 THEN 2020
2080 IF M<0 THEN 2020
2090 IF S<0 THEN 2020
2100 B(K)=D+(M+S/60)/60
2110 IF B(K)>90 THEN 2020
2120 IF Q=1 THEN 2220
2130 IF Q=2 THEN 2150
2140 GOTO 2170
2150 B(K)=180-B(K)
2160 GOTO 2220
2170 IF Q=3 THEN 2190
2180 GOTO 2210
```

```
2190 B(K)=180+B(K)
2200 GOTO 2220
2210 IF Q<>4 THEN 2220
2215 B(K)=360-B(K)
2220 PRINT "DISTANCE "
2221 PRINT "(NEGATIVE IF OUTWARD RADIUS)";
2230 INPUT X
2232 L(K)=X
2234 PRINT
2240 IF L(K)>0 THEN 2270
2250 IF ABS(L(K))<>ABS(L(K-1)) THEN 2220
2270 RETURN
2280 END
```

Day of the Week

This program calculates the day of the week that a given date falls on. It will figure, for example, that December 25, 1985 will be a Wednesday.

You must enter the date in numeric form and in the order of month, day, year. September 12, 1975 will be entered as 9,12,1975, making certain that commas, not slashes or dashes, separate the figures.

Examples:

Cindy's birthdate is March 4, 1953. On what day was she born?

Uncle Lon has an appointment on September 30, 1977. What day does that fall on?

```
DAY OF THE WEEK

(ENTER 0,0,0 TO END PROGRAM)
MONTH,DAY,YEAR? 3,4,1953
WEDNESDAY

MONTH,DAY,YEAR? 9,30,1977
FRIDAY

MONTH,DAY,YEAR? 0,0,0

5 GRAPHICS 0
10 PRINT "DAY OF THE WEEK"
20 PRINT
29 REM - REQUEST USER INPUT
30 PRINT "(ENTER 0,0,0 TO END PROGRAM)"
40 PRINT "MONTH,DAY,YEAR";
50 INPUT M,D,Y
59 REM - TEST FOR END OF PROGRAM
60 IF M<>0 THEN 100
70 IF D<>0 THEN 100
80 IF Y<>0 THEN 100
90 GOTO 360
99 REM - NEED TO ADJUST INPUT FOR CALCULATIONS?
100 IF M>2 THEN 130
109 REM - ADJUST INPUT
110 M=M+12
120 Y=Y-1
129 REM - CALCULATE DAY NUMBER
130 N=D+2*M+INT(0.6*(M+1))+Y+INT(Y/4)-INT(Y/100)+INT(Y/400)+2
140 N=INT((N/7-INT(N/7))*7+0.5)
149 REM - FIND CORRECT DAY NUMBER, TRANSLATE TO DAY, PRINT
150 IF N>0 THEN 180
160 PRINT "SATURDAY"
170 GOTO 340
180 IF N>1 THEN 210
190 PRINT "SUNDAY"
200 GOTO 340
```

```
210 IF N>2 THEN 240
220 PRINT "MONDAY"
230 GOTO 340
240 IF N>3 THEN 270
250 PRINT "TUESDAY"
260 GOTO 340
270 IF N>4 THEN 300
280 PRINT "WEDNESDAY"
290 GOTO 340
300 IF N>5 THEN 330
310 PRINT "THURSDAY"
320 GOTO 340
330 PRINT "FRIDAY"
340 PRINT
349 REM - RESTART PROGRAM
350 GOTO 40
360 END
```

Days Between Two Dates

This program calculates the number of days between two given dates. Leap years are taken into account.

The program assumes there is one day between today and tomorrow. For instance, there are two days between March 1 and March 3 of the same year.

There are a few precautions to assure the proper use of this program. First, you must be certain to enter the earlier date first. Second, dates must be entered in number form (3, not MARCH) and in the correct order (month, day, year, i.e., 3,17,1976). Commas, not slashes or dashes, must separate the figures. Third, the year must not be abbreviated (1976, not 76), even if both dates are in the same century. Finally, the month entered must not be greater than 12 and the days no greater than the number of days in the particular month. If such is the case, the message UNREAL DATE is printed to alert you to the fact that an unreal date (such as 14,32,1975) has been entered. An incorrect answer is likely to result.

Example:

John's birthdate is August 8, 1951. How many days old will he be on his 30th birthday?

```
DAYS BETWEEN TWO DATES

FIRST DATE? 8,8,1951
SECOND DATE? 8,8,1981
DIFFERENCE = 10958 DAYS

MORE DATA (1=YES, 0=NO)? 0

5 GRAPHICS 0
10 PRINT "DAYS BETWEEN TWO DATES"
20 PRINT
29 REM - STATEMENTS 30 TO 60 REQUEST USER INPUT
30 PRINT "FIRST DATE";
40 INPUT M1,D1,Y1
50 PRINT "SECOND DATE";
60 INPUT M2,D2,Y2
69 REM - SET VARIABLES TO BE USED IN SUBROUTINE
70 M=M1
80 D=D1
90 Y=Y1
100 GOSUB 230
109 REM - SAVE COMPUTED NUMBER OF DAYS IN N
110 N=A
119 REM - SET VARIABLES TO BE USED IN SUBROUTINE
120 M=M2
130 D=D2
140 Y=Y2
150 GOSUB 230
159 REM - CALCULATE DIFFERENCE AND PRINT
160 N=A-N
170 PRINT "DIFFERENCE = ";N;" DAYS"
```

```
180  PRINT
189  REM - RESTART OR END PROGRAM? USER INPUT REQUIRED
190  PRINT "MORE DATA (1=YES, 0=NO)";
200  INPUT X
210  IF X=1 THEN 20
219  REM - END PROGRAM
220  GOTO 460
227  REM - SUBROUTINE TO COMPUTE NUMBER OF DAYS FROM 0/0/0/ TO M/D/Y
228  REM - START WITH TEST FOR UNREAL DATE
229  REM - GO TO CORRECT TEST DEPENDING ON NUMBER OF DAYS IN THE MONTH
230  ON M GOTO 260,280,260,340,260,340,260,260,340,260,340,260
240  PRINT "UNREAL DATE"
249  REM - STOP CALCULATIONS, RETURN TO MAIN PROGRAM
250  RETURN
259  REM - MONTH HAS 31 DAYS
260  IF D>31 THEN 240
270  GOTO 350
279  REM - MONTH IS FEBRUARY; A LEAP YEAR?
280  IF Y/4<>INT(Y/4) THEN 310
290  IF Y/400=INT(Y/400) THEN 320
300  IF Y/100<>INT(Y/100) THEN 320
309  REM - NOT A LEAP YEAR; MONTH HAS 28 DAYS
310  IF D>28 THEN 240
319  REM - A LEAP YEAR; MONTH HAS 29 DAYS
320  IF D>29 THEN 240
330  GOTO 350
339  REM - MONTH HAS 30 DAYS
340  IF D>30 THEN 240
349  REM - TABLE OF NUMBER OF DAYS FROM FIRST OF YEAR TO FIRST OF EACH
MONTH
350  DATA 0,31,59,90,120,151,181,212
351  DATA 243,273,304,334
360  RESTORE
361  FOR Q=1 TO M
362  READ A
363  NEXT Q
369  REM - GET NUMBER OF DAYS FROM JANUARY 1 TO FIRST OF MONTH FROM DATA
TABLE
379  REM - COMPUTE NUMBER OF DAYS FROM 0/0/0 TO M/D/Y
380  A=A+Y*365+INT(Y/4)+D+1-INT(Y/100)+INT(Y/400)
389  REM - POSSIBLY A LEAP YEAR?
390  IF INT(Y/4)<>Y/4 THEN 450
409  REM - CONTINUE TEST FOR LEAP YEAR
410  IF Y/400=INT(Y/400) THEN 430
420  IF Y/100=INT(Y/100) THEN 440
428  REM - IF MONTH IS JANUARY OR FEBUARY, ADJUST CALCLATED NUMBER OF
DAYS
430  IF M>2 THEN 450
440  A=A-1
449  REM - END OF SUBROUTINE, RETURN TO MAIN PROGRAM
450  RETURN
460  END
```

OPTION

To shorten this program you may wish to omit the test for unreal dates. It should be noted that if a month of more than 12 is entered when this test is omitted, an input error will result. The program lines which may be deleted are listed following the example below.

Example:

How many days are there between July 4 and Christmas?

```
DAYS BETWEEN TWO DATES

FIRST DATE? 7,4,1977
SECOND DATE? 12,25,1977
DIFFERENCE = 174 DAYS

MORE DATA (1=YES, 0=NO)? 0

1 REM - OPTION 100, 150, 228-340
5 GRAPHICS 0
10 PRINT "DAYS BETWEEN TWO DATES"
   .
   .
90 Y=Y1
100 GOSUB 350
109 REM - SAVE COMPUTED NUMBER OF DAYS IN N
   .
   .
140 Y=Y2
150 GOSUB 350
159 REM - CALCULATE DIFFERENCE AND PRINT
   .
   .
227 REM - SUBROUTINE TO COMPUTE NUMBER OF DAYS FROM 0/0/0/ TO M/D/Y
(Delete lines 228-340)
349 REM - TABLE OF NUMBER OF DAYS FROM FIRST OF YEAR TO FIRST OF EACH
MONTH
   .
   .
450 RETURN
460 END
```

Anglo to Metric

This program converts a measure given in anglo units to metric units. The conversions available in this program are as follows:

1 Inches to centimeters
2 Feet to centimeters
3 Feet to meters
4 Yards to meters
5 Miles to kilometers
6 Teaspoons to cubic centimeters
7 Tablespoons to cubic centimeters
8 Cups to liters
9 Pints to liters
10 Quarts to liters
11 Gallons to liters
12 Bushels to liters
13 Pecks to liters
14 Ounces to grams
15 Pounds to kilograms
16 Tons to kilograms
17 Degrees Fahrenheit to degrees Celsius

You must provide the value of the anglo measurement and the number of the conversion (1 - 17 as listed above) which you wish to perform.

Example:

Perform the following conversions:

8.5   miles to kilometers
75°   Fahrenheit to degrees Celsius
10   gallons to liters

```
ANGLO TO METRIC

(TO END PROGRAM TYPE 0)
WHICH CONVERSION DO YOU NEED? 5

VALUE TO BE CONVERTED? 8.5

8.5 MILES = 13.6765 KILOMETERS

WHICH CONVERSION DO YOU NEED? 17

VALUE TO BE CONVERTED? 75

75 DEGREES FAHRENHEIT
= 23.88888888 CELSIUS

WHICH CONVERSION DO YOU NEED? 11
```

VALUE TO BE CONVERTED? 10

10 GALLONS = 37.85 LITERS

WHICH CONVERSION DO YOU NEED? 0

```
5 GRAPHICS 0
10 PRINT "ANGLO TO METRIC"
20 PRINT
29 REM - ESTABLISH VARIABLES FOR 17 CONVERSION FACTORS
30 DIM C(17)
39 REM - LOOP TO ASSIGN CONVERSION FACTORS INTO C()
40 FOR N=1 TO 17
50 READ X
52 C(N)=X
60 NEXT N
69 REM - DATA TABLE OF SEVENTEEN CONVERSION FACTORS
70 DATA 2.540,30.480,.3048,.9144
71 DATA 1.609,4.929,14.788,.2366
72 DATA .4732,.9463,3.785,35.24
73 DATA 8.809,28.3495,.4536,907.2
80 DATA .6214
89 REM - GET NUMBER OF CONVERSON FROM PROGRAM DESCRIPTION
90 PRINT "(TO END PROGRAM TYPE 0)"
100 PRINT "WHICH CONVERSION ";
101 PRINT "DO YOU NEED";
110 INPUT N:PRINT
119 REM - END PROGRAM?
120 IF N=0 THEN 540
129 REM - CONVERSION AVAILABLE?
130 IF N>17 THEN 100
140 PRINT "VALUE TO BE CONVERTED";
150 INPUT I
152 PRINT
159 REM - PERFORM CONVERSION USING PROPER CONVERSION FACTOR
160 R=I*C(N)
169 REM - DIRECT PROGRAM TO PROPER CONVERSION UNITS, PRINT RESULTS
170 IF N<10 THEN 175
173 ON N-9 GOTO 360,380,400,420,440,460,480,500
175 ON N GOTO 180,200,220,240,260,280,300,320,340
180 PRINT I;" INCHES = ";R;" CENTIMETERS"
190 GOTO 520
200 PRINT I;" FEET = ";R;" CENTIMETERS"
210 GOTO 520
220 PRINT I;" FEET = ";R;" METERS"
230 GOTO 520
240 PRINT I;" YARDS = ";R;" METERS"
250 GOTO 520
260 PRINT I;" MILES = ";R;" KILOMETERS"
270 GOTO 520
280 PRINT I;" TSP. = ";R;" CUBIC CENTIMETERS"
290 GOTO 520
300 PRINT I;" TBSP. = ";R;" CUBIC CENTIMETERS"
310 GOTO 520
320 PRINT I;" CUPS = ";R;" LITERS"
```

```
330 GOTO 520
340 PRINT I;" PINTS = ";R;" LITERS"
350 GOTO 520
360 PRINT I;" QUARTS = ";R;" LITERS"
370 GOTO 520
380 PRINT I;" GALLONS = ";R;" LITERS"
390 GOTO 520
400 PRINT I;" BUSHELS = ";R;" LITERS"
410 GOTO 520
420 PRINT I;" PECKS = ";R;" LITERS"
430 GOTO 520
440 PRINT I;" OUNCES = ";R;" GRAMS"
450 GOTO 520
460 PRINT I;" POUNDS = ";R;" KILOGRAMS"
470 GOTO 520
480 PRINT I;" TONS = ";R;" KILOGRAMS"
490 GOTO 520
499 REM - CONVERT FROM DEGREES FAHRENHEIT TO CELSIUS
500 R=(I-32)*5/9
510 PRINT I;" DEGREES FAHRENHEIT"
511 PRINT "= ";R;" CELSIUS"
520 PRINT
522 PRINT
529 REM - RESTART PROGRAM
530 GOTO 100
540 END
```

Alphabetize

This program alphabetizes a list of words or phrases.

Numbers may be part of an alphanumeric phrase. However, they will not be put into numeric order unless they contain the same number of digits. Numbers with fewer digits must be justified to the right by prefixing zeros. Thus, if the numbers you are sorting range into the hundreds, the number 13 would be entered as 013.

To save memory space, the value of Y at statement 65 should be limited to the number of characters of the longest item you wish alphabetized. The statement should be altered in the following manner:

$$65 \quad Y= L$$

where L = length of largest item to be entered.

Example:

Alphabetize the following names:

    Robert Wilson
    Susan W. James
    Kent Smith
    Michael Mitchell
    Ann T. McGowan
    Alexander Lee II
    Mary Mitchell
    David Bowers
    Steven Evans
    Carol Jameson
    Linda North

```
ALPHABETIZE

(TO END PROGRAM ENTER 0)
NUMBER OF ITEMS? 11
 ITEM 1? WILSON ROBERT
 ITEM 2? JAMES SUSAN W.
 ITEM 3? SMITH KENT
 ITEM 4? MITCHELL MICHAEL
 ITEM 5? MCGOWAN ANN T.
 ITEM 6? LEE ALEXANDER II
 ITEM 7? MITCHELL MARY
 ITEM 8? BOWERS DAVID
 ITEM 9? EVANS STEVEN
 ITEM 10? JAMESON CAROL
 ITEM 11? NORTH LINDA
BOWERS DAVID
EVANS STEVEN
JAMES SUSAN W.
JAMESON CAROL
LEE ALEXANDER II
MCGOWAN ANN T.
```

```
MITCHELL MARY
MITCHELL MICHAEL
NORTH LINDA
SMITH KENT
WILSON ROBERT


NUMBER OF ITEMS? 0

5 GRAPHICS 0
10 PRINT "ALPHABETIZE"
11 REM - CHANGE LINE 65 TO REFLECT CORRECT VALUE OF Y
12 REM - WHERE Y = LENGTH OF LONGEST ITEM TO BE ENTERED
20 PRINT
30 PRINT "(TO END PROGRAM ENTER 0)"
40 PRINT "NUMBER OF ITEMS";
50 INPUT N
60 IF N=0 THEN 330
65 Y=30
70 DIM A$(Y),B$(Y),A(N,Y),W$(1)
80 FOR I=1 TO N
90 PRINT "ITEM ";I;
100 INPUT A$
101 REM - STORE ITEM IN ARRAY 'A'
102 FOR J=1 TO LEN(A$)
103 A(I,J)=ASC(A$(J,J))
104 NEXT J
105 REM - FILL UNUSED CHARACTERS WITH SPACES
106 IF LEN(A$)>=Y THEN 110
107 FOR J=LEN(A$)+1 TO Y
108 A(I,J)=32
109 NEXT J
110 NEXT I
120 M=N
126 REM - THE SORT TECHNIQUE USED COMPARES DATA ITEMS IN
127 REM - DIMINISHING INCREMENTS.  THE FIRST PASS COMPARES ITEMS
128 REM - N/2 ELEMENTS APART, THE SECOND (N/2)/2 ELEMENTS APART
129 REM - AND SO ON UNTIL THE INCREMENT IS EXHAUSTED.
130 M=INT(M/2)
140 IF M=0 THEN 280
150 K=N-M
160 J=1
170 I=J
180 L=I+M
182 REM - CONVERT TWO VALUES TO STRINGS
185 FOR X=1 TO Y
186 A$(X,X)=CHR$(A(I,X))
187 B$(X,X)=CHR$(A(L,X))
190 NEXT X
192 REM - COMPARE THE STRINGS
195 IF A$<B$ THEN 250
196 REM - EXCHANGE IF NOT IN ORDER
198 FOR X=1 TO Y
200 Z=A(I,X)
210 A(I,X)=A(L,X)
220 A(L,X)=Z
225 NEXT X
```

```
226 REM
230 I=I-M
240 IF I>=1 THEN 180
250 J=J+1
260 IF J>K THEN 130
270 GOTO 170
275 REM SORT COMPLETE, OUTPUT RESULTS
280 FOR I=1 TO N
281 REM - CHECK FOR FULL SCREEN (20 LINES)
282 IF I/20<>INT(I/20) THEN 290
283 REM - WAIT FOR OPERATOR CUE TO GO TO NEXT SCREEN
284 PRINT "PRESS 'RETURN' TO CONTINUE";
285 INPUT W$
286 REM VALUES OUTPUT ONE CHARACTER AT A TIME
290 FOR X=1 TO Y
292 PRINT CHR$(A(I,X));
294 NEXT X
296 PRINT
300 NEXT I
310 PRINT
319 REM - UNDIMENSION ARRAYS, RESTART PROGRAM
320 CLR
325 GOTO 40
330 END
```

OPTION

You may wish your list alphabetized in reverse, or from highest to lowest. The necessary program changes are listed following the example below.

Example:

The scores on a math test range from 82 to 117. Put the students in order according to their scores, from highest to lowest.

```
 89    Bowers
102    Evans
111    James
100    Jameson
 99    Lee
117    McGowan
102    Mitchell
 82    Mitchell
 97    North
 91    Smith
108    Wilson
```

```
ALPHABETIZE

(TO END PROGRAM ENTER 0)
NUMBER OF ITEMS? 11
```

```
ITEM 1? 089 BOWERS
ITEM 2? 102 EVANS
ITEM 3? 111 JAMES
ITEM 4? 100 JAMESON
ITEM 5? 099 LEE
ITEM 6? 117 MCGOWAN
ITEM 7? 102 MITCHELL
ITEM 8? 082 MITCHELL
ITEM 9? 097 NORTH
ITEM 10? 091 SMITH
ITEM 11? 108 WILSON
117 MCGOWAN
111 JAMES
108 WILSON
102 MITCHELL
102 EVANS
100 JAMESON
099 LEE
097 NORTH
091 SMITH
089 BOWERS
082 MITCHELL

NUMBER OF ITEMS? 0

1 REM - OPTION 195
5 GRAPHICS 0
10 PRINT "ALPHABETIZE"
   :
190 NEXT X
195 IF A$>B$ THEN 250
198 FOR X=1 TO 30
   :
330 END
```

References

Mendenhall, William, et al. *Statistics: A Tool For the Social Sciences,* North Scituate,
Mass.: Duxbury Press, 1974.

Paige, Lowell J., and Swift, J. Dean. *Elements of Linear Algebra.*
Boston: Ginn and Company, 1961.

Sakarovitch, M. *Notes on Linear Programming.*
New York: Van Nostrand Reinhold Company, 1971.

Spiegel, Murry R. *Theory and Problems of Statistics.*
New York: Schaum's Outline Series, Schaum
Publishing Company, 1961.

Thomas, George B., Jr. *Calculus and Analytic Geometry,*
part one, 4th ed. Reading, Mass.: Addison-Wesley, 1968.

U.S. Department of Commerce, *Handbook of Mathematical Functions.*
National Bureau of Standards, Applied Mathematics Series 55, 1964.

Other OSBORNE/McGraw-Hill Publications